I0542784

WRITING REVERSE HAREM FOR FUN & MONEY

A Rage Against the Manuscript guide

SECOND EDITION

STEFF GREEN

ISBN: 978-1-99-104664-2

❀ Created with Vellum

Chapter One

ARE YOU READY TO WRITE YOUR REVERSE HAREM NOVEL?

Reverse harem books have been tearing up the romance bestseller charts for years now. Although stories about falling in love with more than one person have always been around, the trope of one woman having multiple male partners has been having a moment in the spotlight recently.

And I, for one, am here for it.

Since around 2016, reverse harem has become a common term used by readers to identify a type of book where a heroine acquires a 'harem' of three or more guys who are all utterly devoted to her. Unlike a love triangle where the heroine has to choose one lover in the end, in a reverse harem, she gets her "happily ever after" with all of them.

2017 was the year reverse harem novels really started to tear up the charts, and these romances have gone from strength to strength. Fueled by an active social media presence and an army of voracious readers, reverse harem books are still going strong. In fact, they're more popular than ever.

Reverse harem is no longer a small romance "niche" or a fly-by-night "trend", but another flavor of romance – like MF, MM, or menage. You cannot look at the romance charts without seeing several reverse harem books, and reverse harem novels from Raven Kennedy, Tate James, Nikki St. Crowe, and Angel Lawson and Sam Rue (to name just a few) have occupied the number one spot in the Amazon store.

Readers love these stories because of the wish-fulfillment factor. How amazing would it be to have not one devoted guy at your beck and call, but five? Having more than one hero also enables authors to explore personality types beyond the typical alpha male, leading to more diversity and fun.

When I first wrote Writing Reverse Harem for Fun & Money back in 2019, this upstart genre was on the verge of becoming evergreen. Now, it's evergreen AF. Reverse harem is here to stay and the fans are still demanding more.

For a writer, reverse harem can be an exciting challenge and a great career move. Let's make this clear right now – the smut is way more fun. But more than that, reverse harem can open up some creative possibilities that might not fly in the wider romance market.

The reason I write reverse harem is because I love being able to write different types of heroes. With MF romance – which is what I wrote before 2018 – there can be a certain type of alpha male that you write again and again. I like to mix things up. I'm a sucker for tortured artist-types and neurodivergent men, and kind betas who are quietly devoted. In reverse harem, these characters get their chance to shine alongside more typical alpha males.

I also love the diversity of stories and settings and worlds, and the challenge of creating a situation that would foster this unusual type of relationship.

And, like I said, the smut. OH, the smut!

If you're excited to write your own reverse harem, I've created this resource to pull together some tips and tricks I've learned since I started publishing these books. You're currently reading the second edition of this guide, as I've updated it in 2023 to take into account the changing market, new trends, and visibility tools and techniques (such as Tiktok).

As a six-figure author of several popular reverse harem series (under my pen name, Steffanie Holmes), I'll show you how to craft a story your readers will love, and how to make sure those readers can find your books. I'll give you the best tools to help you reach success, and have fun at the same time.

Are you ready? Let's get writing!

ABOUT ME

Just so you know I'm not talking out my arse, I'll tell you a little about my writing career and success with reverse harem.

I'm Steff, and I've been self-publishing my work since 2014. I started off writing super series science fiction novels in the vein of China Mieville. These sold at the rate of 0-3 copies per month.

One day, I attended a party where a friend and I were discussing *50 Shades of Grey*. This friend loved the books, and I'd read the first chapter and couldn't continue because the writing style and grammar didn't appeal to me.

I was having a bitch about this book's success, when my friend cut in to say, "It's not as if you could write a sexy book like that, Steff."

She meant that she thought I was too sweet to write sexy romance, and I nodded in agreement and changed the subject, because of course she was right. In my group of very sexually adventurous friends, I'm known for being quite private about my sex life and, well, I can't say the word 'penis' without blushing. But in my head, the cogs were turning.

Challenge accepted.

In secret, without telling anyone, I wrote a 30,000-word

story about a fox shapeshifter named Ryan who lived as a reclusive artist, and the gallery curator, Alex, who brought him out of his shell. There's a shifter war and an unhinged brother and a crumbling medieval manor and all sorts of intrigue. I paid $50 for a cover and published it in April 2015 under a secret pen name – Steffanie Holmes. I expected nothing to happen except that one day when I wasn't so mortified about the sex in it I could show it to my friend and we'd both have a laugh.

I sold 1000 copies in the first week.

I couldn't believe it. I kept expecting Amazon to call me to say they'd given me someone else's royalties by mistake. But they never called and the sales kept coming. I had to sheepishly tell my husband that I'd made all this money from my books, but it wasn't from science fiction, it was from this smutty fox shifter romance story.

After he got done laughing, he said, "So, are you going to write more?"

Fast-forward to 2023. I've published over 50 books in total, most of them paranormal or dark, gothic contemporary romance novels as Steffanie Holmes. I quit my day job in Feb 2018 in order to live the dream life of a full-time writer. I earn six-figures a year from my writing and have the most incredible fun doing it. I am so insanely lucky and grateful and that's why I've written this guide – because I want you to be able to share in the joy of telling stories of the heart and seeing your writing find an audience.

MY REVERSE HAREM BOOKS

A week after I left my day job, I released my first reverse harem novel, *The Castle of Earth and Embers,* book 1 of the Briarwood Witches series. Up until this point, I'd been doing well off the back of my previous paranormal romance novels, but it's thanks to this series that my career took off.

Before the book's release, I was earning between $1000-3000 per month on Amazon, and about $1000 on the other stores. Since I started releasing the Briarwood Witches books, my income climbed to $4k, $6k, $10k, and up.

I released 5 books in that series throughout 2018, approximately 1 book every 2 months. In December 2018, I released the box set of the complete series.

In January of 2019, I released book one in my new Nevermore Bookshop Mysteries series, *A Dead and Stormy Night*. What's been interesting about this series is that it doesn't follow the typical conventions of a romance book. I planned it based around a cozy mystery plot, but with reverse harem elements. It was a gamble, but that gamble paid off – the Nevermore Bookshop series was even more successful so far than the Briarwood Witches, and it's so much fun to write. Interestingly, the series took off again in 2022 thanks to Tiktok, and it's become my third bestselling series ever. It's my fan favorite series and probably what I'm best known for.

In May 2019, after three Nevermore Bookshop novels were out, I published book one in a brand new, dark paranormal series called Kings of Miskatonic Prep. I happened to write this book right as the bully romance trend was happening, and so I had a huge amount of reader interest in this series simply based on the blurb for book 1. This series (which is paranormal, when most bully books are contemporary) hit the top 20 on Amazon and was such a wild ride! I tripled my monthly income and I thought I had this self-publishing lark all figured out.

Over 2020 and 2021, while the pandemic raged, I wrote more reverse harem (and one menage duet) – I wrote mainly contemporary books. Basically, I was trying to replicate the success of Kings of Miskatonic Prep with the dark bully audience, and mostly not succeeding. I wrote an incredibly successful dark bully series in 2022, which made me realize...I was done writing dark bully. Oh dear. Sometimes we have to learn these things about ourselves the hard way.

In 2023, I returned to my first love – paranormal and fantasy. My Grimdale Graveyard Mysteries series is part of the same world as Nevermore Bookshop, and it's proved even more popular than the early series. I've got so many more books planned – a mixture of MF and reverse harem, and I'm still madly in love with being a writer and creating worlds.

Throughout this book, I'll be referring to all my series, as these are readily available sources for examples. You might like to read them to see how I put the lessons in this book into practice in order to create a six-figure income from reverse harem. I'll also refer to other reverse harem books, which you'll find in the suggested reading list at the back of this guide.

Chapter Two

WHAT IS A REVERSE HAREM ROMANCE?

I discovered reverse harem as a reader in 2017. I'd been hearing the phrase pop up in writing conversations for a few months, but I wasn't that interested until a writer friend raved about the Rock Hard Beautiful series by CM Stunich. A rockstar romance where the girl ends up with the whole band? That's my kind of story!

I devoured the three books in that series over the weekend and went hunting for more. What I discovered was not a one-off wonder but a whole world of unique settings, strong female characters, and harems of guys who worship them.

I joined groups on Facebook dedicated to discussing all things reverse harem and discovered that the trope actually started in anime, manga, and otome games. In reverse harem anime, the girl has a group of guys who exist around her (and may or may not be in love with her). In the end, she has to choose one of them. Some of the best reverse harem anime are *Uta no Prince-sama!, Fruits Basket,* and *Ouran High School Host Club.*

Some women watching or reading reverse harem anime and manga got sick of the idea of the girl having to choose between all the guys. Too often you'd end up hating the guy she actually did choose or wishing it was a different kind of story altogether. These fans had also been reading *Twilight*, *The Hunger Games,* and other popular YA genre fiction with love triangles and wishing Bella and Katniss didn't have to choose. They probably also secretly read the smutty books of Laurell K Hamilton (whose popular vampire series is one of the earliest reverse harem stories). All these things came together to create the bubbling cauldron from which reverse harem was born.

We've read too many love triangles over the years and we're tired of seeing the Jacobs and Gales of the world miss out.

What if the heroine didn't have to choose?

Guys in stories got to have harems of women who all share, so why couldn't it work in reverse?

Some of those fans started writing their own stories where the female main character didn't have to choose. Early writers like CL Stone and BL Brunnemer self-published their work (they definitely have an anime influence in their story structures and character mannerisms). These series took off and readers demanded more more more. Other authors noticed this going on and started writing their own stories with heroines who had their happily ever after with three or more heroes and didn't have to choose. While Stone and Brunnemer's books were glacially slow-burns, with no steamy scenes at all or much later in the series, newer books tended to be steamier, as the authors writing them came from the world of steamy paranormal or contemporary romance. At some point, readers started referring to them as 'reverse harem'.

This started reverse harem as a book genre/flavor of romance.

Reverse harem readers are greedy – they want it all. All the guys, all the feels, all the sex, all the heartbreaks, and heartthrobs. They love reverse harem in all its different facets – some of the books are aimed at a young adult audience, with teenage protagonists who might not even kiss until book six (CL Stone, B L Brunnemer). Others are hyper-steamy with the sexual tension and bedroom acrobatics turned up to 11 (CM Stunich, Tate James, K A Knight, Angel Lawson, AK Rose, Steffanie Holmes...)

In the early days, most reverse harem books were paranormal. This was in part because it's easier to create a paranormal setting where having more than one "mate" is socially acceptable, and in part because to start, the audience for these stories came from anime and YA paranormal books like *Twilight*. There were always a few contemporary reverse harem books around (one of my favorites being Bethany Jadin's series, The Code), but in 2019, reverse harem books started landing in the top 100 contemporary books – the most competitive romance subgenre.

Now, in 2023, with readers and authors finding their tribes over on Tiktok, contemporary and paranormal reverse harem books are popular, and fantasy romance (especially darker fantasy) with reverse harem is having its moment in the spotlight.

There are reverse harem books in every imaginable romance genre – historical, fantasy, science fiction. Many reverse harem books cross over with non-romance genres, such as urban fantasy, cozy mystery, and psychological thriller.

In the early days, people wrote reverse harem off as a trend that would rise and die within 6-12 months. Now, reverse harem is an important part of the romance landscape.

I love this because it helps to normalize polyamory and different types of relationships. Many reverse harem books involve elements of queer representation and often tackle difficult issues as characters struggle to come to terms with being who they are. I also love the diversity in the books and how they showcase something many people might consider kinky or creepy as truly beautiful and life-affirming.

Let's dive into the unique elements that define reverse harem. Just a note before we begin:

I am a professional author. Writing is how I pay my mortgage and keep my cats in the manner to which they've become accustomed. Because of this, I come at the genre with an eye to what is going to sell. The title of this book is *Writing Reverse Harem Romance for Fun AND MONEY.* The money part is as important to me as the fun part. If it's not for you, then feel free to ignore everything I say and write whatever you like. But if you're like me and you want to strive to find an audience, sell books, and perhaps even become a full-time author, then filter your ideas through the information I give about where the market is right now and what readers expect.

ELEMENTS OF A REVERSE HAREM NOVEL:

First up, let's take a birds' eye view at the reverse harem market and discuss some of the common features of these stories. This chapter will give you a good, strong trunk from which to sprout your ideas.

Point of view: Most reverse harem books are written in first person, with alternating point-of-view (POV) chapters. Most of the chapters will be from the heroine's POV, with some from the guys.

I love this structure – particularly in enemies-to-lovers

books, where you can see into the guys' heads as they torment the heroine that they're more conflicted than she ever realizes. Readers love having the guys' voices in the story.

Single POV from the heroine only is also relatively common, although I'd say less so now than it was in the early days.

A few reverse harem books are in third (Alex Liddell's *Power of Five*, for example – although this combines 1st and 3rd POV), but third is definitely not the norm and I wouldn't personally choose it. The romance market as a whole has moved from third person to first person and readers are more used to first person than they have ever been before.

Tense: Past and present tense are both common. I would say that present tense has become significantly more common in recent years. In contemporary romance in particular, present tense is the norm.

I'm not talking about future tense.

Series or standalone: There is more variation in series structure now than there used to be, especially now that reverse harem has become big in contemporary romance.

I'd say that most reverse harem novels follow a typical fantasy series arc with the same characters battling an external conflict as they deal with their internal conflicts. Each book in the series follows the same heroine and her harem and ends with a cliffhanger, and reverse harem authors take great pride in making those cliffhangers as wild and rage-inducing as possible (I know I do). All my series follow this format, whether they are contemporary or paranormal or fantasy.

This series format works in the genre for a number of reasons:

- With so many main characters to wrangle, a series allows you more space and more words to explore their internal and external conflicts. (You just need more SPACE to tell a satisfying romance story).
- Writing a series means you can finish books quickly and have more new releases than if the same story was one giant standalone, and this can be better for visibility in the Amazon store.
- The cliffhangers create great sellthrough numbers between books – much higher than that of unlinked standalones or interlinked standalones.
- Book one can be a loss leader. You can lose money advertising it and still come out with a decent profit because of the sell-through between the later books in the series.
- Readers follow characters across several books, and this often creates a bond with your story world that produces lifelong fans.

And, for some clarity, here are the disadvantages of writing a reverse harem series:

- This biggest disadvantage is that if the series is a flop, you're left with the difficult choice of having to follow through and finish all the books or start on something new and leave the story unfinished.
- You can lose your motivation and love for the characters while writing the series, especially as new ideas bite you on the arse.
- Authors tend to love writing the first couple of books in a series, and find the latter books a slog (I know that I do!) This often means authors will begin several series at once and will then have

whole years where all they're doing is writing
difficult final books to finish all their projects.

Less common is the traditional romance series format of a
series of interconnected standalones – where a new couple is
introduced in every book. I think this is because it's much
harder to weave a satisfying romance arc for a heroine *and*
three or more heroes in one book, and then connect that to
another character who also wants a reverse harem relationship. Some authors (such as Stephanie Brother) have had
success with this model, but I wouldn't personally use it as I
think it has all the disadvantages of series and standalones
without a lot of the advantages. It's simply not as fun for me,
and the fun part is as important as the money part!

Standalone novels – a complete story wrapped up in a
single book – are becoming more common in reverse harem. I
think KA Knight's *Den of Vipers* showed readers and writers
what could be achieved in a standalone book. Roxy's story is
raw and dirty and ridiculous and so fun.

Pro tip: With so many main characters and relationships
to juggle, standalone RH novels tend to be massive tomes, so
only embark on writing one if you're prepared to spend the
rest of your life signing a literal brick!

Advantages of standalones:

- One and done. The story is complete in a single
  volume. This means that you can move on to a new
  story – can work well if you struggle to follow
  through with a longer series.
- If the book is a flop, you're not locked into writing
  more in that world.
- A massive tome = a massive payout in Kindle
  Unlimited page reads.

- The shorter format may inspire you to try something a little riskier that you might not want to do for a full series.

Disadvantages of standalones:

- The biggest disadvantage is that sellthrough between standalone books by the same author is significantly worse than books in a series. This is because readers are series-loyal first, genre-loyal second, and author-loyal a distant third. There is a lot you can do here to increase sellthrough, such as setting standalones in the same world and using cameos of beloved characters to connect them, but sell through is always going to be a struggle because once the readers are done, they're more likely to move onto another author's books than your backlist.
- It's more difficult to get a positive ROI on advertising a standalone. Not impossible, but more difficult.
- If a book is a success and you want to double down, you might not have anywhere else to go to expand the world and offer readers more. There are heaps of things you can do here, but if you haven't planned for this, it can often be less successful than you hoped.

Ultimately, how you choose to structure your book and series are up to you and the story you want to tell.

Female heroine: A reverse harem novel wouldn't be complete without a heroine to be the center of the world. She's the protagonist, and she's the one who drives the story.

She's also the one around which all the guys (who may not always get on with each other) rally.

Reverse harem protagonists come in all shapes, sizes, and personalities, with endless variations of emotional baggage and character wounds. I thought I'd use this section to talk about some of the traits I notice most often in popular RH books, and why they work well with this genre.

Reverse harem protagonists have a lot of inner strength. You have to be strong to handle this many male egos!

The heroine has an equal amount of love for all of the men because each of them fills a particular emotional need. For example, in my Briarwood Witches series, Maeve needs Corbin in order to bounce ideas off and puzzle out the mysteries of Briarwood Castle, while Arthur helps her to realize her inner strength.

Your heroine probably has a dark past that leads to relationship issues – an abusive household, sexual assault, grief, etc. She's hurting, but she might not realize it yet. Her men are going to help her to heal herself, and her love will heal them. A lot of popular RH books have zany, OTT plots that often include a ridiculously dark past for the heroine (especially in the dark contemporary books).

She might be hesitant to love, especially to love more than one guy. She doesn't know what to do or how to choose. This will likely be an initial source of conflict in your book.

Because most reverse harem books are new adult (characters aged 18-25), the heroines tend to be more innocent than you'd perhaps see in books with older characters. Heroines are often (but not always) virgins, and even if they are badass fighters or mages like many protagonists of urban fantasy and paranormal RH, they tend to be innocent in other ways.

Readers are often harsher on a heroine than any of the heroes. (Heroes can be *literal serial killers* and still be hot, but if the heroine is too whiny or a bitch, then you better believe you'll hear about it). I believe this is because when readers enjoy these books, they "imprint" themselves on the female protagonist, and so they don't like to imagine themselves as having these negative traits. This is something I try to remember when I'm writing my heroines. They can be flawed, and they can go on an inner journey, but their character has to feel relatable the whole way through the book. A heroine who needs to overcome past trauma inflicted on her by someone else in order to be with her men is a common theme in popular books.

3 or more heroes (aka, the harem): You want three or more love interests for your heroine to collect. The number you choose is up to you. Most reverse harem books include 3-5 heroes, but some have many more. (CM Stunich's *Harem of Hearts* series includes nine!) Remember that the more you have, the harder it might be to give each of them a satisfying emotional arc. Also, if you're writing explicit sex scenes, then more than four guys might leave several heroes without anything to do! I'm personally a fan of 3-4 guys, but you do you!

Make your guys as distinct in looks and personality as possible. Here, you're able to step outside the typical romance alpha male heroes and explore other personality types, so take advantage of that. This is the main reason I enjoy writing reverse harem so much. I always have two super alpha guys, and then at least one guy who is a bit "outside the norm" – I love beta guys, tortured souls, protectors, outlaws, nerds, jokers, poets, guys who aren't conventionally attractive, guys with physical disabilities or mental health struggles, etc.

Also, think about the romance tropes you want to write, and create your heroes to fit those. For example, enemies-to-lovers and bully romance work well with alpha hole, morally-gray heroes. What about a stepbrother romance? What about a mafia/arranged marriage trope? What about growly, protective wolves and fated mates? With heroes, your job is to pick a trope that readers already love and then use the conventions of that trope to make them fall utterly in love with your hero.

Many authors like to look at Jungian archetypes or Myers-Briggs personality types to compose their heroes. This can be heaps of fun!

Usually, the guys already have some kind of relationship in the beginning of the book. In my Nevermore Bookshop Mysteries, Heathcliff, Morrie, and Quoth have been living together as friends before they meet Mina. In BL Brunnemer's Veil Diaries series, the guys are all high school friends who 'adopt' the heroine, Lexie. In KT Strange's Rogue Witch series, the guys are all werewolves and all members of the band Phoenixcry. However, that doesn't mean you can't throw in a surprise or two. In Briarwood Witches, four of the guys are close friends, and I throw in a random stranger, Blake, at the end of book 1 to shake things up. Not all of the guys accept Blake right away, even though the heroine Maeve bonds with him. This type of conflict keeps the reader glued to the page.

Romance plot: Reverse harem books are romance books.

Let's say that louder for the people at the back.

Reverse harem books are romance books.

The people who read these books read romance. They are familiar with romance tropes. They know what they want from a romance story.

This means your RH book needs to follow the structure, themes, and tropes of a romance. You may include elements of other genres (most commonly, reverse harem books cross over with urban fantasy, but there are also epic fantasy, science fiction, steampunk, mystery, thrillers, gothics, and more.) but at their core, these should be romance stories with a happily-ever-after.

When thinking about your story, it can help to think about it in terms of the tropes you want to write. You can combine a couple of tropes because you have three or more heroes to play with.

My bestselling 2022 series, *Stonehurst Prep: Elite*, is a dark bully romance with the stepbrother trope, as well as morally-gray villains as heroes, gang/mafia romance, and a decent dose of "Who did this to you?"

Usually, a romance novel will have external and internal conflict. For example, in a dark, bully romance, the heroine is at a school on scholarship and she has something to prove, so she won't back down even when the three hottest guys in school decide she's public enemy number one. And the three guys want to drive her away because their families hate her for something that happened in their past or because she threatens to usurp their leader's place as top of the class or something like that. That's external conflict. This external conflict might have echoes of other genres – it might be a mystery arc, like in my Nevermore Bookshop series, or a fantasy arc, as in Raven Kennedy's Plated Prisoner series. But this plot needs to serve the romance between the characters, not the other way around.

But then you have internal conflict – this is what's going on inside the characters' heads, even and especially when they don't realize it. Each of the three guys are falling for the heroine but each has some deep character wound (usually stemming from something that happened in their childhood) that means they sabotage their happiness. The heroine has her wound, too.

For one guy, it might be that his sister died when he was little and so he's terrified of loving someone again because they'll leave him and he'll hurt. For another, it might be that he's hiding part of himself from his family (perhaps he's supposed to take over the family business but he really wants to be an artist) and he's afraid of getting close to someone because that means admitting to himself that he's hiding.

I don't know about you, but for me, these wounds are the most fun part of the story to write, especially when they crash up against the heroine and the other guys in the harem.

We'll talk more about plot and conflict and wounds and all that good stuff in a later section.

Common tropes: Reverse harem is a flavor of romance, and romance readers are all about devouring their favorite tropes. If you want your reverse harem book to be successful, you should pack it full of tried-and-true romance tropes and fantasies.

A trope is a common theme or motif. Tropes might be a situation (marriage of convenience / only one bed), they might be a type of character or character relationship (enemies to lovers / grumpy/sunshine), or they can be a wider "theme" that encompasses several tropes in a specific way (for example, "bully" romance, which is enemies-to-lovers with a specific power dynamic AND a specific setting AND specific character types). Often, certain tropes go together well for maximum fun – enemies-to-lovers works well with forced proximity and only one bed, and grumpy sunshine and friends to lovers are excellent bedfellows.

In romance books, tropes are used to bring together the lovers and to throw up conflict between them. Tropes are also the coat rack from which readers hang their fantasies. That's why we read romance, after all – to escape into a fantasy! For romance readers, tropes become popular because they perfectly encapsulate or fulfill a fantasy. For example, "billionaire whisks perfectly ordinary heroine away from her boring life into a whirlwind of luxury and debauchery" is a popular trope because women are often responsible for taking care of everyone around them, so having a guy make all your problems go away is a fun fantasy.

In reverse harem, tropes can sometimes apply to the heroine's relationship with only one of the guys, or with all of them. For example, I've written a number of bully romance series where the bully aspect is only between the heroine and one or two of the guys, not the whole haren.

Many readers have favorite tropes, and certain tropes are eternally popular. Also, tropes are something that can trend. For example, as I'm writing this, "hockey romance" is a trend, as is "dark fantasy romance featuring capturing and arranged marriage." We had a "magical academy" trend a few years back, and a "rejected mates" trend. And the "monster romance" trend. Trends are always changing and they're never what you expect!

How do you know which tropes are popular and what readers expect from them? You need to be a reader of romance novels. For example, even though I hadn't read a stepbrother RH before I started writing *Poison Ivy*, I had read enough stepbrother romance books to know the expectations. In the first scene, our heroine has a one-night stand that absolutely blows her mind and makes her question what she's done with her life. Because she never intended to see this guy again, she is completely uninhibited and does things she never imagined she'd do.

In the next scene, she has to go and meet one of her parents who announce they're getting married, and her parent's new partner introduces their son. Of course, it's the cocky god from her wild night. Now, they have to live together, or go on a family holiday (forced proximity) with the memory of that encounter hanging between their every interaction. Often, there's an enemies-to-lovers aspect, too, usually around one or both of them hating their parents getting remarried. And you know that eventually, they're going to...

That's what I, as a reader, expect. So that's what I wrote into *Poison Ivy*. Only one of the characters is her stepbrother, but I made sure that his part of the story included all the gooey, delicious, tropey goodness that readers expected.

A reverse harem is still a romance. The most successful reverse harem books rely on tried-and-true romance tropes. If you're writing reverse harem for money, as well as fun, then starting with tropes is a good way to go.

Whychoose: In a reverse harem book, the happily-ever-after involves the heroine settling into a relationship with *all* her guys. If she chooses a single guy – or some plot point puts all the other guys out of the picture – then it's not a reverse harem, and you'll end up with a lot of upset readers and bad reviews.

Reverse harem readers also expect a story where the members of the harem focus on the heroine – the world revolves around her. Sometimes, men in the harem may also have MM relationships with each other. This might be a relationship that existed before the heroine came on the scene, or it might be a deepening of a connection they've been denying, or a new thing they explore. You have to be careful here that these MM relationships still make the reader feel as though the heroine is the center of the story – she can't be a bit on the side while they navigate a true romance with each other. There's no data on this, but I'd say around 50% of the RH books I read have MM relationships (and around 50% of the RH I write, too). Some readers don't like MM content and specifically avoid it, but you'll find enough who expect and enjoy it that including it won't kill your sales.

For examples of how it can be done well, check out Britt Andrews' Emerald Lakes series and CM Stunich's Hard Rock Beautiful series.

Remember that a reverse harem story is a particular type of polyamorous relationship, and readers expect this specific type of relationship. They expect loyalty to the heroine from all of the guys. An exception can be made for an MM relationship within the harem, as long as the heroine is still centered in this. The guys can't have other partners outside the harem (I'm sure there are exceptions to this rule that have done well, but mostly they flop because they don't meet reader expectations).

A polyamorous relationship where every member of the harem can have multiple partners is a different type of book. If you're writing this, you're not writing reverse harem. The fantasy of reverse harem is having three or more men who can fulfill every physical and emotional need you can possibly imagine, and who adore you and you alone. It also leans heavily into the found family trope.

HEAT LEVELS AND SEXY TIMES

Let's talk about sex! (Because of course, why else would you have purchased this book?)

Like all romance novels, reverse harem books come in all different heat levels. Imagine heat levels work on a scale of 1-5. 1 is hand-holding and maybe a chaste kiss, and 5 is lighting the bedroom on fire. At heat level 5, the characters live their emotional journey through sex, with multiple and explicitly-described sex scenes.

Let's break those heat levels down:

- Level 1 (Clean/Sweet/Chaste): Think PG-rated movies. In a level 1, you might have some hand-holding, maybe a kiss, but no below-the-pants stuff and definitely no dirty thoughts or sex toys flying around.

- Level 2 (Mild steam): You get some sexy feelings, intimate moments, and hot kisses, but they are brief and described mainly in terms of emotions instead of booties smooshing. Most physical intimacy happens off the page. The reader doesn't get to be inside the character's head for the whole shebang. Lots of kisses and a bit of touching, and some conversation about sex. Sex might happen, but not in front of the reader.
- Level 3 (Medium steam/sexy): The middle ground. Most of us steamy writers live around here. Expect sexy times where you get to live inside the heroine's head and feel what she feels, both emotionally and physically. The sex scenes primarily serve to further the emotional arc of the characters, and will only appear when they can do this.
- Level 4 (Explicit/Scorching): This is where things can get a little kinky. In level 4 we have graphic sex and sexually-adventurous characters who want to try it all. Because of the group scenes in reverse harem, it's likely most of our books automatically get kicked up to this level. Nothing is left to the imagination, and that's the way we want it.
- Level 5 (Nuclear): This is the level at which the emotional arc of the characters is linked to their sexual experience, so the whole story plays out between the sheets. Explicit language, explosive sexual tension, and probably lots of kink. Also, not a lot of external, non-sexy conflict. This is all about the world between the sheets.

Reverse harem readers use heat levels when talking about books. They also talk about 'burn' levels. You'll see this come up in reader groups and in Tiktok comments all the time – "Is this a medium or fast burn book?"

This 'burn' is the amount of time it takes the heroine and her heroes to stop dancing around each other and move their relationship to the next level. In its simplest terms, it's the amount of time between meeting and shagging, but it can also refer to sexual tension in general. There are three burn levels:

- slow burn, where it takes several books before any kissing or petting takes place,
- medium-burn, where there are sexy times in book one but maybe not full-on sex or maybe only with one member of the harem to start with, and
- fast burn, where things go from 0 to NC-17 in a matter of minutes!

The majority of successful reverse harem books have a heat level of between 3-5 and are medium burn. Most of them include the heroine enjoying one-on-one sexy times with each of her guys, but will also include group sex scenes where all characters are in bed together.

I'd say, particularly in contemporary romance, books are currently trending spicy and faster burn, but by the time I proofread this book and put it up for sale, this may have changed!

Most of my reverse harem series have a heat level of 3-4 and are considered medium burn. I have one series with a sex scene in the first 3 chapters, but most of them have sex in the later half of book 1, although the full harem tends not to be introduced until later books. I have group scenes in all my series because as a RH reader myself I love those scenes, but I do read some books where there aren't group scenes. I find the majority of RH books are medium burn, with some popular books in the last few years being very spicy (such as *Den of Vipers* by KA Knight, which has essentially a sex scene every chapter.)

Two notable slow burn, low heat series are the Veil Diaries by BL Brunnemer and the CL Stone's Ghost Bird and Scarab Beetle series. These books are young adult in tone and contain building romantic tension between characters, but no sex at all or not until several books into the series. Reverse harem readers call these books slow burn or super-slow burn, and they love them just as much as the more explicit books. Our wonderful readers truly do love it all.

(Although, it's worth noting that both those series came out in the early days of reverse harem, when readers didn't have as many options. Nowadays, I think it would be more difficult for a series with this slow burn/low heat to gain momentum. Not impossible, just difficult.)

Wherever you fall on the spice scale, make sure your heat and burn levels match the tone of your story. If your characters are in their twenties, you probably want a heat level of at least 3. You don't have to include group scenes, especially if you're not comfortable writing them. Some reverse harem novels only include one-on-one sex between the heroine and her harem members.

However, keep in mind that most reverse harem readers choose these books *because* they want the group sex and that group connection. Think carefully about how you're meeting reader expectations when considering how to plot your sex.

Sex scenes – even group scenes – serve a vital purpose in your book. They aren't just there to titillate the reader (that's erotica). Your sex scenes are a vital part of the romantic and emotional arc of your story. If you remove them, the story should be nonsensical.

Tips for reverse harem sex scenes:

Even if you're experienced at writing sex scenes, it can be

intimidating to get hot and heavy with all these different people. If you're worried about too many cooks in the kitchen, try these tips:

- **Read widely:** Read group sex scenes and spicy RH books written by other authors and notice how they... er... tackle the situation. You'll learn more from reading and observing than you will by setting yourself rigid rules.
- **Choose words for all the bits:** Think about your character's history and what words they might choose for all the sexy bits. Avoid purple prose, like 'love rocket' or 'flower'. Stick with the basics – cock, dick, pussy, shaft, etc. Keep it simple and let the emotions drive the scene. Beware of the word cunt as many readers don't like it (although sometimes it's perfect for the character).
- **Build the emotion:** The best sex scenes are all about releasing emotions. Use sex at key points in your plot as your characters become vulnerable and their physical desires get all mixed up with their wacky emotions. At the end of a sex scene, you can leave the characters (and the reader) feeling wrecked and more unsure of themselves than ever. Never leave them 100% satisfied, or they'll put the book down.
- **Think about birth control:** I believe as authors we have a responsibility to represent safe sex. You don't need to say much. The 'rustle of a condom wrapper' is enough to indicate what's going on. You can also use birth control as a plot point – for example, in Briarwood Witches, Rowan's insistence on condoms even after all the harem has been tested is a clue about his tragic past.

- **Build tension:** A sex scene doesn't begin with one of the guys kissing the heroine or removing her blouse. It actually begins much earlier in the book. Use suggestive conversation, dirty thoughts, teasing, touching, kisses, bullying, body language, shyness, and other tools to build sexual tension through your entire story. Make the reader *beg* for that first scene.
- **Try from the male POV:** Switch things up by writing a scene from the POV of one of the heroes. Readers love being inside a man's head while he's worshipping a woman in bed.
- **What are all those guys doing?** You might need to choreograph your scene to keep all your boys busy worshipping your heroine. How can they touch/kiss/caress/penetrate her in various ways? Maybe two of them are in a relationship with each other, so they can stay busy while the others tend to their woman?
- **Keep the same style/tone:** Make sure your characters' personalities are as evident in the bedroom as they are throughout the book. Sex can reveal a lot about who a person is.
- **Surprise your reader:** The unhinged, possessive alpha hole is a total teddy bear in bed and loves cuddles? The shy, quiet guy is a secret dom? Surprise your reader with a bedroom reveal that will make them fall even deeper in love with the heroes.
- **Your heroine should have agency:** Even though the sex in reverse harem is all about the heroine, she shouldn't just lie there and passively take her dicking. Don't fall into the trap of making the sex about the woman 'letting' these men have her

body. Find ways for the woman to take charge, give enthusiastic consent, speak what she wants, and be involved as an active participant in her own pleasure. She likes to give as much as she enjoys receiving.

- **Change it up:** Some sex is quick and dirty because your characters just can't keep their hands off each other. Sometimes, the lovemaking is slow and languid. Sometimes sex is about loving the other person, sometimes it's releasing tension. Sometimes it's losing yourself in sensation, or forgetting a horrible event, or seeking solace in a warm body. Sex can be in a bed, in the back of a car, in an empty classroom, under the stars... There are so many possibilities! Change up your sex scenes, the combinations of people, and the emotional drivers in order to keep readers interested.
- It doesn't have to be all or nothing. Sex scenes can be more than just DinV. Think about kinks, about masturbation, about sex that doesn't involve penetration.

Pro Tip: When I write sex scenes, I use my skeleton drafting method (https://www.rageagainstthemanuscript.com/skeletondraftcourse) to fast-draft the scene first. In this first draft, I include some basic actions – what's happening, who's doing what to each other, and in what order. It's like stage directions in a play. However, what I'm really focusing on is the emotional story of the characters. This initial draft includes lots of dialogue and internal thought. Once that's done, I go back over the scene a couple of times and add in the description to make it extra sexy.

To MM or not MM

Even if you tightly plot your reverse harem sex scenes, you might still end up with a few guys waiting their turn. What are they going to do? Maybe they'd enjoy playing with each other...

Many reverse harem books include MM – male/male action. It's by no means essential for a reverse harem story (and some readers actively avoid books containing MM) but it adds another interesting element to the mix if you're willing to give it a try.

Personally, I think that with so many guys getting naked together and being okay with sharing one girl, it makes natural sense that at least a couple of them are also bisexual or pansexual and attracted to each other.

MM works best when it arises as part of each character's emotional arc. It has to feel natural to the reader, not forced.

In a reverse harem it's vitally important that the heroine remains at the center of the relationship. All things – including male/male sexytimes – must flow from her. Often, this is an unspoken attraction between two men who have known each other for years, and when the heroine becomes part of their world, she brings all these feelings to the surface until they...explode. :)

In Briarwood Witches, Rowan has loved Corbin secretly ever since Corbin brought him into the coven. He sees Corbin as kind of a savior figure. But it's not until Maeve comes to the castle that her presence splits open Rowan's wounds and gives him the strength to reveal his feelings for Corbin. Maeve is able to bring the two together. The relationship is more special because they share it with Maeve, and all their key emotional moments happen while she is present and involved with both of them.

FF (female/female relationships) is far less common in reverse harem stories. Generally speaking, readers of reverse harem are straight. They enjoy MM because they like sexy men and they love the vulnerability of men being emotionally open to each other, and that's what makes MM scenes hot. But they don't feel the same way about FF. They don't generally like seeing the guys with another girl. It's silly, yes, and I personally would love to see more FF and more women as a part of a harem, but we're talking about writing for fun *and money*. Generally speaking, the money is *not* in adding a woman to your heroine's harem.

Chapter Three

PLOTTING YOUR REVERSE HAREM

In this section, we look at how to craft your reverse harem story from beginning to end.

No matter the genre of your story, the core of your reverse harem should focus on the relationship arc between the heroine and her men. In popular series that mirror the subtle deepening of feelings shown in Japanese anime (Veil Diaries, Ghost Bird), this relationship develops slowly over time from a friendship group. In other stories, sex might come first, and a relationship develops from proximity or attraction into deep love. Enemies to lovers is also an extremely popular trope and relationship type.

No matter how you write your reverse harem story, it needs to follow the conventions of a romance plot.

For me, one of the biggest ways I've learned about plotting is to read the work of other authors and dissect how they build conflict, create lovable but flawed characters, and increase tension through a book. I suggest you take a look at the reading list at the back of this guide and read a few other reverse harem books to see how the experts do it.

Let's dig into plotting your reverse harem.

SERIES OR STANDALONE

Before you start plotting, it's good to know whether you're writing a single story or a series. You can flip back and re-read the section about series if that helps you make your decision.

My advice is – write a series. Because you're creating a full romance arc for the heroine with **each one of her heroes** – as well as throwing buckets of external conflict her way, and adding a decent dose of worldbuilding (especially if it's fantasy/paranormal) – a standalone book may be 150,000+ words!

While several authors have had hits with amazing standalone reverse harem books, the majority of reverse harem writers create a series.

And that series will be told in an epic style – the story of one heroine and her harem across multiple books, with each book ending on a cliffhanger. These cliffhangers hook readers and leave them begging for the next book in the series. I've used this series structure in all my reverse harem series – I personally love spending so many books with the same characters and am always so sad when I write THE END on the final book and have to let them go.

You should consider plotting your reverse harem story as a series in this way. Here's why:

- Readers expect series and may feel your book falls short of their other favorites if the story is too short.
- You may struggle to fit a satisfying emotional arc for each character in the harem within a single standalone book.
- If you hook readers in book one, you'll make more money on a series than with an equal number of standalone books. Readers binge-read series the

way we binge-watch our favorite TV shows. If they dig your first book, they'll stick around for more.

- Series are easier to market, as you're able to make a loss offering book 1 for free or $0.99 and making up sales on sell-through of the later books.
- You can bundle your series together into a boxset, which can be a lucrative addition to your backlist.

How long should a series be?

- The 'writing for fun' answer: As long as it needs to be to tell the story you want to tell.
- The 'writing for money' answer: At least 3 books, with a longer series if it's doing well.
- The 'what's right for you?' answer is somewhere in between.

The length of your series comes down to a number of factors. How do you prefer to write? Can you shorten/lengthen the series depending on sales of the earlier books?

I'd say that the most common length for a reverse harem series is between 3-5 books. However, there are some as short as two books and some as long as 14+. When planning the length of your series, consider the story you want to tell, and any potential 'out' you want to give yourself if the series isn't selling.

When I planned the Briarwood Witches series, I knew from the beginning I wanted to tell Maeve's story over five books. This was in part because I wanted each book title to relate to one of the five elements of the coven's magic – earth, fire, water, air (wind), and spirit.

When I planned the Nevermore Bookshop Mysteries, I was careful to give myself an 'out', because the idea was a little unusual and I wasn't sure how well the series would sell. It's a cozy mystery/paranormal reverse harem mash-up and I had no idea how my readers would receive it. I decided that if the books weren't selling, I could wrap up the overarching mystery arc in four books. Luckily, they've been my best-selling series to date, so I've been able to continue the series beyond those initial four books and stretch out the mystery. I wrapped up the main mystery in 6 books, but I continued the series for three more books (plus a novella) – although the final 3 books are kind of an extended epilogue that ends in a wedding.

With both my Kings of Miskatonic Prep and Stonehurst Prep series, I originally planned each series to be 3 books, but while working on the series, I realized that I needed an extra book, so each of these series ended up being four books in total.

Long series are amazing because they can be extremely profitable even if book 1 costs more to promote. For example, my Nevermore Bookshop Mysteries series is one of my top-selling series even though its ranks are never as good as other books, simply because the series is so long.

Angel Lawson and Samantha Rue have an incredible dark romance series called Royals of Forsyth University. Book 1 is *Lords of Pain*. They have a college with five fraternity houses who each choose a woman to effectively be their "queen". They write a trilogy about one heroine and the fraternity who choose her (the first trilogy is the Lords, the next is the Dukes, then the Princes, etc...) but they all tell one long, continuous story so they will constantly add new books to the series. Every element of their series and branding has been carefully designed to grow an insane fanbase who clamor for the next book, and it's working for them!

Some writers would get too bored writing a long series.

Some writers can't shut up. :) You have to decide which kind of writer you are.

Long series tend to be more common in paranormal romance, where the stakes can involve saving the world. If a contemporary romance series is longer than 4-5 books, it's usually because the main characters have their happily ever after and a new set of characters are introduced. This can be a great way to extend a series once it becomes popular.

WORD COUNT

When it comes to word count, it might help you to have an idea in mind of the range you want to hit, but make the book as long as it needs to be – no longer, no shorter. Word count is not generally the deciding factor in a book's success, but it can have an impact on the complexity and depth of your story, and the amount you earn if your novel is in Kindle Unlimited.

Because most reverse harem books are sold as ebooks with no printing cost, you have a bit of flexibility with word count. For a standard reverse harem romance novel in a series, you should be aiming at between 50,000-80,000 words per book.

Why this number? This is the standard length for a typical romance book. Your readers are used to this length. Amazon displays a page count on your book's product page where readers can see it. Some readers have a bias against books that are below 200 pages in length. 50,000 words should get you safely over 200 pages – your book will be quick to plot and write without feeling too short. 80,000 words should get you over 300 pages if you want to show readers that your book is longer.

If your book is longer, it will take you more time to write, so you won't gain the benefits of releasing faster. *But* if you're enrolled in Kindle Unlimited, you'll earn a higher amount per book from a full read (more on this later).

Plenty of popular reverse harem books are much longer than 50-80k. Most of my books are 80,000-100,000 words. My books *Poison Ivy* and *Poison Flower* are 140,000 words each. CM Stunich – one of the most popular RH authors around – regularly writes books with around 150,000 words. Caroline Peckham and Susanne Valenti, Tate James, K A Knight, and Angel Laweson and Samantha Rue are all authors with highly successful books in word counts from 120k and up. Longer books give readers more content and more depth into the characters, more sexy times, more angst – just more of everything they love. The KU reads also help!

On the other end of the spectrum, some authors have success writing short serials of 10-20k words and releasing these installments quickly as ebooks (1-2 times per week). Each 'episode' of the serial ends on a cliffhanger, like a TV show. These are more popular in fantasy genres than in romance and there aren't many super successful reverse harem serials (this might simply be because there aren't yet many reverse harem serial writers).

If you're interested in serial writing, it would be worthwhile to check out Kindle Vella as an option. There are also apps like Radish, Galatea/Inkett, and Chapters. All of these enable you to publish serials a chapter at a time. Authors like Nikki St. Crowe and Emilia Rose have been doing insanely well on these platforms, and are also directing their readers to sign up for Patreon and Ream accounts where readers pay the author directly to receive books a chapter at a time as the authors write them. (Nikki St. Crowe is also interesting to look at if you write shorter books generally as she's had a lot of success with shorter novels).

Some authors, like Selena and AK Rose, also write Kindle Vella serials alongside their main books as a way to diversify their income from writing. You don't have to choose one or the other!

All these authors do well because they have figured out what they like to write and they focus on doing that thing well. Don't force yourself to write shorter or longer just because you think it's a path to success.

By all means, create a serial if this is your preferred type of story – and definitely look at Vella and the apps as a viable option to get it off the ground and find an audience. But in general, full-length novels will outsell serials.

THE ROMANCE PLOT

Now, we get into the nitty-gritty of planning and writing your reverse harem story.

Every romance book follows a similar plot related to the emotional journey of the characters. Different authors will break down this plot in different ways. I've written my version below, adapting it from a single MF romance to a reverse harem story.

The important thing to understand about a romance book is that characters aren't just passive onlookers who have a story thrust upon them. Characters *are* your story – it's their desires, hopes, and dreams that create your plot. This is true in all genres but *especially* true in romance.

When creating your story, try not to worry too much about the plot itself. Instead, focus on the emotional journey of the characters.

What does this emotional journey look like? Let's take a look at the stages:

1. THE MEET

The meet is the initial hook/set-up of the story, where the heroine meets her lovers. The reader understands that there's an attraction, but also that the characters can't be together yet because of internal struggles and/or external conflict. This is where your tropes come into play. For example, in an enemies-to-lovers romance, the rivalry between characters prevents them from being together. This rivalry might have an external motivation (eg. destroy the new girl in CM Stunich's *Filthy Rich Boys*) but it's likely motivated by the internal emotional damage of all the characters. (We must destroy the new girl because she makes us confront ugly parts of ourselves and we can't have that).

If possible, your heroine should meet one or all of the harem members in the first chapter. This might not work with your story and is not a hard-and-fast rule. But your heroine's meeting with the harem should happen as early as possible in the book.

During the meet, you might introduce your heroine and each of her heroes separately. She'll probably meet one of them first, then the others, but not necessarily. During this stage, we begin to understand each character's longing – the thing in the book that they believe they need. This might be a dream job that will pull their family out of poverty, or a magical talisman to bring their father back to life, or to overcome their grief or shyness, or to close themselves off to anyone who might care about them so they don't have to feel pain, or just to survive high school. We might see those needs clashing against each other as our heroine and heroes experience conflict.

What's important at this stage is to ensure that your heroine and all their heroes have a **longing**, and they also have a **wound**. Their wound prevents them from achieving what they long for, even though they may not realize it them-selves yet.

The wound is often related to the longing. It can often be the flip side of that longing.

Different characters may long for the same thing, placing them in opposition to each other. This is common in enemies-to-lovers – both the heroine and a member of her harem want to be top of the school – and creates all that juicy conflict we love.

In Briarwood Witches, Maeve meets Corbin in the first chapter, at the fairground where her adoptive parents are killed. She then re-meets Corbin a few chapters later, when she discovers he's one of the tenants in the castle she's inher-ited. She meets the other guys in this chapter, aside from Blake, who she doesn't meet until the very end of the book.

Corbin is trying to hold a coven of male witches together. All he wants is to see his friends achieve their dreams. But his wound is that he doesn't believe he's worth caring for, so he puts everyone else in his life before himself.

Maeve's longing is to get to MIT to study to become an astronaut. Her wound is that she is a person who has found a lot of solace in science because it explains things and makes her feel secure in the world. She was adopted by hyper-reli-gious parents and didn't always feel like she was secure because she knew that her real parents didn't want her. So when she discovers magic is real, it shatters all her beliefs about science and makes her feel unsafe again.

All of this angst is super fun to play with in the story!

2. THE DESIRE

Here, we see what the heroine and heroes are striving for, and understand that even though they cannot see it now, they can't have what they want because of their particular wounds.

We see the heroine's attraction to the heroes and their attraction to her, and understand that this attraction is somehow impossible or forbidden.

The meet and the desire are often mushed together or swapped around.

In Briarwood Witches, we learn about Maeve's desire right from the beginning – to go to college, study physics, and become an astronaut. However, she can't achieve this goal until she reconciles her logical mind with her supernatural powers and learns to stop seeing the world in black/white, right/wrong.

While Maeve is living in her new castle with the guys, you see their desire blossom because she is vulnerable and feels unsafe, and they help her to feel safe again.

3. FIRST TURNING POINT

This is where the characters start to strive for their longing. In a reverse harem romance, the plot will primarily focus on the heroine's longing, or on a collective goal for the harem. However, each character will also have their own longing.

The characters cannot achieve their longing, however, because their wound holds them back. This might manifest as either an external 'baddie' (the antagonist) thwarting their plans or internally as a conflict that holds them back.

At this stage, it's impossible for your characters to achieve their longing.

In Briarwood Witches, you see this as Maeve wanting to sell the castle and go to university. She can't do this because of her inability to embrace her powers and get rid of the fae that are attacking the castle. She can't believe in magic, and so the magical world (the external plot/antagonist of the fae) won't allow her to leave.

4. RAISING THE STAKES:

This is where shit gets real.

The heroine and heroes deepen their relationship. They move closer toward their longing. They see what life could be like after they've achieved it. There's a real shot at happiness and acceptance and all that good stuff.

However, you (the author) still know how impossible this is, because the characters are living a lie. They haven't overcome their wounds. They're hiding things from each other. They're still vulnerable and scared. And the external problems or the real world are closing in. Their wounds are still pushing them back.

In Briarwood Witches, this is the entirety of books 1-3. Again and again, Maeve and her harem strive to return Briarwood to normal, but everything they do just makes their situation ever more dire, and drives wedges between their burgeoning relationship.

5. THE POINT OF NO RETURN

This is another turning point, but it's different from the others because it's at this point that the characters have learned so much about themselves that they can't go back to the way things were before, even if they tried. In some books, they do try, but it's impossible because they're no longer the same people.

This is often where one of the first sex scenes in a romance book will be, or a very emotional sex scene.

Your heroine and her heroes have not yet overcome their wounds, but they're starting to see that that's what they have to do. In Briarwood, the point of no return is actually when Maeve meets her mother, and how that happening changes the relationship she has with her harem. It changes what she thought she knew about family. The actual return of Maeve's mother from the dead is also a *literal* point of no return – now that she's been brought back Maeve can no longer deny the role of magic in her life.

6. BLACK MOMENT

This is when the heroine and the reader believe that all is lost. Maybe the harem has broken up, or they believe there is no way to win. This has to be a true crisis without an obvious or easy solution, or the reader will feel cheated.

Everything explodes as the characters come face-to-face with their wounds in the ugliest and most harrowing way.

In a normal romance book, the black moment is when the two protagonists realize that they can never be together, and they break up, and it's absolutely heartbreaking. They lose all hope in love. They might also be in danger or involved in another crisis, but the key issue is that they don't believe they can have their happily ever after.

In reverse harem books, the black moment can be difficult, because you have 3+ heroes with different wounds and they all need a black moment with the heroine. It can be hard to make that work. Here are some ways RH authors tackle the black moment:

- The heroine has a black moment with members of the harem individually throughout the series, but they will come together during the climax to face some final external struggle.
- The black moment may be with only one of the heroes, but you have to establish that without this hero, the heroine doesn't see her relationship as complete, even if the other heroes are on her side. The heroes might take her side or his, and this can

create additional conflict. I did this with Claudia and her guys in my Stonehurst Prep series – she fell out with Eli, but it made her believe she had lost all of them.

- The black moment may be an external issue – they are together and strong, but there is no way they can defeat their enemy, so they will die (and dying isn't generally considered a happily ever after). I see this often in reverse harem books. CM Stunich's Rich Boys of Burberry Prep series has this kind of ending.
- The black moment may be with all three of the heroes because of the heroine's wound. I find this hard to do but I have seen it done well.
- The black moment may be a sacrifice, where the heroine gives up her harem because she believes this will save them, or the harem gives up the heroine so she can have a better life without them. This is one of my favorite endings to use.

What is the absolute worst thing that could happen to your heroine and heroes? Usually, this is related to the trauma that created their wound. Bring back their worst enemy. Show them how history will repeat itself if they carry on with the relationship. Take your characters to a black moment that is their own personal nightmare, and see what they're made of now that they've found love.

A misunderstanding as a black moment is common, but it tends not to be a favorite with readers. Authors tend to feel drawn to a misunderstanding between characters because it means that no one has to be the bad guy, but when done right a black moment isn't about anyone being the bad guy – it's about two people succumbing to the trauma of their unhealed wounds…and then love finding a way to heal them fully. If you want to satisfy readers with an amazing ending, then you need a truly satisfying black moment.

In Briarwood Witches, each of the men has their own black moment throughout the series, but the final black moment belongs to Maeve. She needs the strength of all five of her men in order to find the strength to do what she has to do.

The main black moment is Corbin's death. The coven believes they are strong, but when they lose Corbin they discover that all their strength came from him, and not from themselves. They fall to pieces and it seems impossible for there to be any happiness without Corbin.

7. THE DARK NIGHT OF THE SOUL

The dark night of the soul usually comes after the black moment. It's when all seems lost and your protagonists must confront what Eckhart Tolle calls "a collapse of perceived meaning."

Some craft teachers consider the black moment and dark night of the soul as the same thing. Personally, as a romance writer, I believe they are two different things – the black moment is when everything falls apart (when the couple splits up), and the dark night of the soul is a personal moment with the protagonist where they realize that they are the reason everything has turned to custard. They are too late to fix things.

This is the point when your character makes the decision to finally heal their wound. Often, this also means giving up their longing and doing something that's more in line with their true self. Or sometimes it means achieving their longing but realizing it doesn't mean anything to them any longer without their love. It may mean they figure out how to have both by following a path they didn't see before. Or they may choose to go after the antagonist on their own. It may be a sacrifice, but it is a sacrifice they can only make now that they have healed their wound.

This is a scene or chapter, or even a couple of paragraphs, where the heroine must reflect on her mistakes and what she has lost because of them. The heroes must have their own dark night of the soul, as well. But you may not show all of theirs in different POV chapters.

Force their bad decisions down their throats and lay bare who they truly are. They can't move forward until they fully accept and own the consequences of their wounds.

8. THE CLIMAX

This is the point of the book where the heroine and heroes face their final challenge, only this time they have moved past their wounds and are now fully their true selves.

In a romance novel, the climax often takes the form of a grand gesture by the heroes – this is a female fantasy, after all, and sometimes we just want someone we love to swoop in and save the day so we don't have to do everything ourselves :)

I love to do the climax as the heroine going off to fight the big bad or deal with a challenge on her own. She's doing this because it's the right thing to do and because she has learned the strength to believe in herself, even without the guys around. But at the last possible moment they appear (in the audience while she gives her big speech, or beside her as she's fighting a demon. Or perhaps she shows up at the place and they're already there). They have come to stand beside her because they love her. Together, they complete the final challenge.

(Sometimes, the black moment, climax, and dark night of the soul occur all at the same time, or slightly out of order).

9. HAPPILY EVER AFTER

The heroine uses her own skills and the support of her harem to save the day. Or the harem realizes how much they need the heroine and fly in at the last moment to save her. Hooray!

What happens next?

It's the bit romance readers LIVE for – the happily-ever-after. There's an emotionally-satisfying conclusion and everyone kisses and apologizes, and usually there's a marriage proposal (but not always).

(Marriage proposals in RH are a unique issue because in most places a marriage between four or more people isn't legal. Sometimes, the heroine will marry one guy (usually for some kind of benefit, like an inheritance), but make a commitment to all of them. Sometimes they'll have a "not-wedding" ceremony. Sometimes there will be a fantasy world where a marriage between more than two people is the norm. Have fun coming up with your own creative solution.)

The happily ever after can only happen when the heroine and every member of their harem overcome their wounds to be together. That's why the black moment and dark night of the soul are so important. Often, it is the strength of the bond of the harem and their love for the heroine that heals the men.

The happily-ever-after also includes some kind of resolution of the protagonists' longings. For example, if someone longed for a specific career, then they might achieve this. Or if they longed for forgiveness for a mistake that cost their sibling's life, then they will get this forgiveness (If it's a fantasy, perhaps they will visit the dead and get this forgiveness from the sibling themselves).

For example, Maeve and her harem each uncover their own hidden strength. They travel to the underworld, save Corbin, and find a unique solution to the problem of the fae.

Each member of the harem has their own happily-ever-after – not only in love by being with Maeve, but also by uncovering and celebrating their strengths in new ways.

Pro tip: remember that with several heroes in the book, your heroine might reach a turning point with different characters at different times. This helps to keep the tension mounting during the series – just when one relationship seems rock-solid, another character has a crisis. Conflict is what makes a series interesting, and in reverse harem, you can pack a mountain of conflict into a tiny book!

REVERSE HAREM PLOT/CHARACTER CONFLICT

If your characters meet, have sex, fall in love, then live happily ever after, your readers would be bored. A story needs conflict in order to get the reader to invest in the characters and grow attached to their struggles.

Think about what's going to cause conflict in your story. Here are some common plot and character themes from reverse harem books that can be sources of conflict. This is not an exhaustive list, but it might stimulate some of your own ideas. You might like to include:

- One of the guys resists the idea of being part of the harem. He doesn't want to share the heroine, and part of his character arc is to release this possessive urge. I use this for Arthur in the Briarwood Witches series, and Cassius in *Poison Ivy*.
- The heroine is the 'chosen one' for some kind of magical society, with special powers she doesn't know she possessed. She has to learn how to use these powers, and her guys are her guardians or teachers.

- The heroine may reject her powers and try to live a normal life. The guys may be tasked with capturing her and returning her to her new (or old) life.
- The heroine needs magic/power/love from an outside source in order to reach her full potential. Usually, that source is one other person, but for some reason there's an accident/fault, and now it's several people. She may deal with societal pressure and ostracism because of this.
- The heroine is royalty/important/upper class and in need of protection by a band of soldiers/guardians. These types of novels use the forced proximity trope and often deal with forbidden romance between different classes.
- The heroine is captured by a group of secret agents/cops/criminals, who she comes to care for. These are often dark romances featuring dub con (dubious consent) and Stockholm syndrome.
- Revenge – the heroine may be seeking revenge for a wrong done to her, and hires or uses the guys to help her do it, or she may be taking revenge on the guys and accidentally falls for them instead. CM Stunich's *Filthy Rich Boys* or Cora Lee June's *Lies and Other Drugs* use revenge as a key theme.
- They fall first – this often goes hand in hand with friends-to-lovers or enemies-to-lovers tropes. The heroes fall for the heroine long before she even notices them. Perhaps they fell for her years ago. This leads to one of my favorite types of scenes – where she confronts them about their weird behavior (maybe she thinks that they don't like her anymore) and they scream, "It's because I'm utterly in love with you," and then kiss her until she

forgets to breathe. I used this with my character of William in *Pretty Girls Make Graves*.

- Fated mates – the heroine experiences a magical connection to the men in her harem, and must come to terms with their world, which will be new to her. Fated mates are common in shifter stories, and often deal with animal instinct vs higher thought.
- Rejected mates – a subset of fated mates, whereby the heroine is rejected by a potential mate. In some stories, the mates who rejected her will reform and come around and become her harem. But in most rejected mates stories the heroine finds herself in a new harem of men who appreciate her for who she is.
- Arranged marriages – a cultural or religious tradition/family obligation ties the heroine to a group of men. Usually, these are also enemies-to-lovers stories where the heroine starts off hating the heroes and then grows to love them through shared adversity.
- Fairytale retellings – traditional fairy tales, legends, and myths are twisted and retold with a reverse harem bent. These stories are rife with family conflict and magical worlds colliding. Check out Marie Robinson's *House of Secrets* or Nikki St. Crowe's The Never King for great examples.
- Forbidden romance – there are a few common forbidden romance tropes. The most common ones are a stepbrother romance (AK Rose's Blood Ties series uses this), teacher/student (plenty of academy romance series have one teacher in the harem, including the Kings of Quarantine series by Caroline Peckham and Susanne Valenti, and the

Mate Games series by K Loraine and Meg Anne.
Age gap relationships are another one, as are
relationships between different races/creatures in
fantasy novels (if you create a world where they
cannot be together). My personal favorite type of
forbidden romance is with a Catholic priest, but
there definitely aren't many of those around!

- Fish out of water – the heroine struggles to fit in at
  her academy, workplace, court, etc, which provides
  a ton of conflict. Usually, there is a power
  imbalance here – she might be a poor girl at a rich
  school, a peasant girl elevated to princess, or a new
  employee with a demanding boss. The guys
  become her friends and confidants and help her to
  navigate this world she's found herself in, or they
  start off as her bullies and are the source of
  conflict.

- The heroine was friends with the boys when they
  were all children. For some reason, they are all
  separated and find each other again as adults.
  Sparks fly, but the reason they were separated will
  haunt them. See Eva Chase's *Witch's Consorts* series
  or many dark bully series.

- Bully romance – The heroine is selected as a target
  for a group of bullies. They have a specific reason
  for choosing her – perhaps their families are rivals,
  or maybe she saw something she shouldn't, or
  perhaps they have to choose someone as part of an
  initiation. My personal favorite story for a bully
  romance is when the heroes are messed up from
  their own trauma, and they believe hurting her is
  the only way to save her and drive her away. I use
  this in my bestselling Kings of Miskatonic Prep
  series.

Pro tip: Usually, the heroes in a reverse harem novel already know each other. They may be friends, bandmates, soldiers in the same unit, or part of a tribe or pack. This makes it much easier for you to set up the story and move on to the meatier parts of the book.

In other books, the heroine acquires the guys one-by-one, or a combination thereof. In my Briarwood Witches series, Maeve meets four of her five men when she first arrives at Briarwood Castle, and they've already forged a deep friendship. The fifth guy, Blake, is a witch raised by the fae who follows Maeve back from the fae realm. His trickster ways and the fact that he was raised fae means the other guys distrust him. Even though Maeve accepts him into the coven, it takes the others time to befriend him.

COMMON TROPES

We've already spoken a little about tropes in reverse harem, especially in the last section. Tropes are themes and devices used in a plot, and they're often the key to uncovering the conflict in your story. In romance, tropes are usually used to bring the characters together or create a conflict in their impending relationship. There are lots of common tropes that readers love and actively look for.

You can combine reverse with other common romance tropes for maximum conflict and readability. Readers unfamiliar with reverse harem will be more likely to pick up your book if it deals with another common romance trope, and you improve your chances of success. Certain romance tropes also go in and out of fashion, and if you happen to write a book that focuses on a trending trope, you may find that readers gobble it up!

What are some common romance tropes you could use in your reverse harem story?

FORCED PROXIMITY

Characters who can't stand each other or are completely different are thrown together with no way out except to cooperate.

You need a reason why all these characters are thrown together and why the guys choose to focus on this one girl. Often, there's a paranormal/magical reason for the connection – in KT Strange's Rogue Witch series, Darcy is a witch working as a band manager who is forced to manage the werewolf band Phoenixcry. Throwing these two feuding magical races together on a tiny tour bus is the heart of the story's initial conflict.

ENEMIES-TO-LOVERS

This trope often goes hand-in-hand with forced proximity. The sparring leads of the novel realize they have the hots for each other. Hatred and passion combine on the page and the result is explosive. Enemies-to-lovers is perhaps the most common romance trope I see in reverse harem, but it's also because I love it as a reader so I probably pay more attention to books that use it.

BULLY

A bully romance is basically enemies-to-lovers in a school setting, only with a power dynamic. For some reason, the heroes – the most popular guys in school – have decided to ruin the heroine. Sometimes this is done through outright bullying and pranks and breaking her, sometimes it is some sort of dare or challenge to date her and make her fall for them and then reveal that she was tricked. However, unknownst to the guys, as they go about their campaign of terror, she is the one who is actually breaking them down, exposing their flaws, making them vulnerable.

What usually happens in a bully romance series is that the first book is the heroine being utterly destroyed, the second book is her revenge, and it's during the process of her getting her revenge that they all realize they're into her (they fall first), and they grovel for her forgiveness and then use all their cruelty and malice to then defeat her ultimate enemy, whoever that may be.

Bully is one of my favorite tropes to read, and I've written a few before, too (Stonehurst Prep, Stonehurst Prep: Elite, Kings of Miskatonic Prep, Dark Academia). Bully often crosses over with dark mafia/gang romance, where the heroes are actually in some kind of gang or are involved in criminal shenanigans.

Bully has been extremely popular in contemporary reverse harem for at least four years now. It's been getting darker and darker, but there are definitely a lot of writers out there doing it well, so it's also very competitive.

MAFIA/GANG

Mafia is basically billionaire romance but with an edge. The guys are hot and loaded and the rules don't apply to them, but they're also part of the criminal underworld that rules whatever city where your books are set. You do not have to be accurate to the real Sicilian mafia in order to write a mafia romance. It can be your own world with your own crime families. They do not have to be Italian. Russian mafia (Bratva) are popular, as are rich and powerful crime families from any background.

Gang romance is kind of the same thing, except usually it's a bit grittier and dirtier and "on the ground" then the mafia romance where the guys are behind the scenes, calling the shots. Bea Paige's Academy of Stardom series and CM Stunich's The Havoc Boys series are both gang romances.

Arranged marriage and kidnapping stories are very popular within these types of books. We are seeing more women rising to the top of crime empires, too – this is a trope I've used in my Stonehurst Prep and Stonehurst Prep: Elite series.

Also check out J Bree's Hannaford Prep and Tate James' Shadow Grove world of novels for mafia/crime romance.

CHILDHOOD FRIENDS/HOMECOMING

The heroine and her guys were friends as children. For some reason, they are separated (perhaps the heroine moves away, or their parents forbid them to talk to each other, etc). They meet again as adults and their childhood friendship blossoms into romance. However, whatever tore them apart the first time still threatens their love. Eva Chase has two series – Witch's Consorts and Gang of Ghosts – which use this child-hood friends theme.

Sometimes writers can add a dark twist to this and turn them into childhood friends to enemies to lovers – this is popular in bully romance. Bea Paige's Academy of Stardom series uses this trope with our heroine, Pen, being friends with the guys when she was younger, only to be forced to betray them. Years later, she meets them at the academy only to find that they still hate her, although over time that hate blossoms into love...

PSYCHO HEROES

This is a trope that's become insanely popular thanks to Tiktok, mainly because the platform loves a shock twist, and these heroes provide that. Psycho heroes are guys who have no problems killing, maiming, torturing, or doing whatever it takes to keep their girl safe and happy.

The favorite psychos might be terrifying to everyone else, but around their girl they are a total kitten. They will treat her like a queen and do anything to make her happy.

These guys love to take revenge on anyone who hurts their heroine, and they often do it in imaginary ways. They are a revenge fantasy, pure and simple, so have fun with that. Psycho heroes are usually the most devoted of the harem, and they're a great character to include as one of a group to make the writing fun.

Probably the best example of a psycho hero (and one everyone STILL talks about, Is Diezal from K A Knights Den of Vipers. This guy is a complete psychopath but from the very first moment he is utterly devoted to Roxy. And the sex with psychos is always hot and raw and usually a little bit freaky.

FORBIDDEN LOVE

This is your classic Romeo and Juliet tale. The children of warring families fall in love, or your heroine and heroes are of different classes or races. There might be other reasons, such as societal taboos, which I spoke about in the last section.

Whatever the reason, their relationship will bring a world of trouble down on their own heads, but they cannot stay away from each other.

FAKE RELATIONSHIP/MARRIAGE OF CONVENIENCE

This is a super popular trope in historical romance books and some contemporary romances. I see it a lot in billionaire/mafia/rockstar romance (those are all the same things, btw – mafia is billionaire with danger. Rockstar is billionaire with music and drugs.) Originally, it wasn't very big in reverse harem, but thanks to Tiktok, it's had a bit of a resurgence in recent years. A marriage of convenience might be difficult, but you can have a lot of fun coming up with a plot around a heroine having to have a fake relationship with 3+ guys at once!

In this trope, the heroine and hero/es agree to pretend to be in a relationship for mutual benefits (usually monetary or to get other family members off their back). However, during the course of this fake relationship, they uncover real feelings for each other.

MAGICAL ACADEMY

This is more of a fantasy trope than a romance trope, but it's popular in reverse harem so I've included it in the guide. In an academy book, your heroine finds herself in an elite, magical school. She has to navigate the politics of this new academic system and its students (who inevitably hate her), with the heroes as her allies/adversaries. For a great example, try *Wishing for them* by Ellabee Andrews or the Phoenix Academy series by Lucy Auburn.

Magical Academy books (paranormal/fantasy) have different tropes and expectations to new adult bully or new adult high school or college romance (contemporary). It pays to read a bunch of them to see what readers enjoy. They may have a bully romance aspect (See Eva Chase's Royals of Villain academy) but there are other expectations too, beyond the bully plot.

Other common tropes in romance are blackmail, best friend's sibling, arranged marriages, class warfare, guardian/ward, kidnappings, mail-order brides (I don't see this in RH very much to be honest, but I might be looking in the wrong places!), falling through a portal, revenge, or the secret/lost heir to a throne or mighty fortune.

Common character types for heroes are athletes (hockey romance is insanely big right now), jocks, artists, billionaires, cowboys, soldiers/guardians, royalty, vampires, werewolves (and other shapeshifters) fae, and other supernatural creatures.

Pro tip: In the early days, most reverse harem novels have some kind of paranormal element. It was easier to set up a harem if there was a magic-based reason for it to exist.

If you're writing contemporary novels set in the real world, it can be more difficult to figure out scenarios where a harem might develop (and how the members can have their happily-ever-after).

You may find it easier to have all the guys be a group from the start. Look for groups of men who might normally co-exist together, especially if they exist outside the norms of society – roommates, band members, stepbrothers, sports teams, colleagues, Navy SEALs, motorcycle gangs, doomsday preppers, etc.

Chapter Four

MARKETING YOUR REVERSE HAREM BOOK

One of the reasons I think my reverse harem books have done well is because I'm a fan of the genre first, and a writer second. I didn't start writing these books to make a quick buck – I poured my heart and soul into creating stories that are incredibly personal to me and that (I hoped) would make readers happy.

When it comes to marketing my series, a lot of what I do is second-nature because I already had a small audience from my previous MF books and I was already talking about reverse harem books as a reader in the largest Facebook groups. Back when I started in RH, the core reader group for this genre was still small, so if you involved yourself in the community early on, you stood the best chance of engaging them with your book when it came out.

That's no longer the case. Reverse harem is firmly established as a flavor of romance in its own right. RH books are frequently seen in the top 10 in the Amazon store and have taken the number one spot numerous times. The audience is growing every day and with so many options for books to read, it's harder to be visible. But that doesn't mean you can't find success — far from it!

In this section, I've included some tips on marketing your reverse harem series, and I've updated it for 2023. I've included topics like your title, cover, blurb, and launch strategy - but this is definitely not an exhaustive list. I hope it will give you some idea of what has/hasn't worked for me.

PRE-LAUNCH

What do you need to do before you launch your reverse harem book in order to give it the best possible chance of success? Let's find out:

CHOOSE YOUR PEN NAME

The first step is to decide on the name to author your reverse harem.

You might like to use your own name. However, if you have conservative relatives or are concerned about what work colleagues might say when they discover your books, you might consider using a pen name.

Each pen name you have (and many authors have many) should encompass books that appeal to the same broad audience. That way, your readers won't be surprised by sudden changes in genre. If it's romance and the heat level is similar, you can include it under one name.

Remember, a pen name isn't just the name on the book — it's a brand. A pen name is a promise that you make to your readers. "Books by this author will give you THIS experience." The more clearly you define that experience and then use every tool you have to give the readers that experience, the more successful you'll be and the more rabid your fans.

See my course on Rock Your Author Brand for an in-depth strategy on creating a successful pen name and author brand: https://www.rageagainstthemanuscript.com/rockauthorbrand

(Use the code REVERSEHAREM to get $20 off)

I have lots of opinions about brands and pen names and all that jazz. Basically, here's where I land.

Authors like us tend to read widely. Readers don't. Readers as a general rule – especially the readers we're targeting with our super tropey KU books – enjoy one genre and that's pretty much it. This can be hard for us to grasp but it's important to understand when we're making decisions about our marketing strategy.

Readers are series-loyal first, genre-loyal second, and author loyal a distant third. Readers won't in general read everything you write just because you wrote it. The authors they *are* loyal to are those who give them the same experience over and over – so they know exactly what they're getting when they pick up one of that author's books. The author keeps a promise to their readers.

The more you jump around vastly different genres, the more you break this promise. The reader can't trust you. This means they will be less loyal and unlikely to swap around your different series.

So pick a thing and stick to it. This means picking romance. This may mean picking the same "vibe" of romance (eg. paranormal or dark contemporary or rom coms, but some authors do mix these successfully, including me). I fundamentally believe this means picking a certain heat level and sticking to it.

Do you need a specific pen name just for your reverse harem books? My answer is, it depends.

Romance readers are so used to seeing reverse harem books now that I believe those who aren't into them simply skip over them for the MF books. Most RH romance readers also read MF, and many read MM. For this reason, I launched my own reverse harem books under my established paranormal romance pen name. Many, many authors mix MF, MM, RH, and other types of romance successfully under one pen name. It's more important for the heat level and general "vibe" of the books to all be similar. The tighter the branding, the more readers view the name as a trusted source and the more you'll be able to pull them between series.

However, if your current pen name publishes outside the romance genre (or a romance-adjacent genre like urban fantasy), I'd consider starting a fresh name. You don't want your young adult thriller readers getting confused!

REVERSE HAREM OR WHYCHOOSE?

You may have seen discussions online about whether these books should be called 'reverse harem' or 'whychoose'. Whychoose was an alternative hashtag for reverse harem books that has been around since the early days, but has never been as popular or as well understood.

A couple of years back, AMS stopped allowing ads with the word 'reverse harem' to be advertised. 'Whychoose' became an alternative that could signal to the reader that this is the type of book they'd enjoy and would also sneak past Amazon's censor bots in your subtitle or description.

Amazon has since become wise to this and 'whychoose' is also banned in your metadata.

Some readers on Tiktok have pointed out that reverse harem could be seen as offensive to Islamic culture. They suggest using whychoose instead. There is a lot of debate about this and even Islamic readers cannot agree if it is offensive or not.

No one wants to offend anyone, so I totally get the caution here. I'm not from Islamic culture, so I cannot give an informed opinion.

What I can say is that, at the time of writing (March 2023), reverse harem is still the dominant way that readers understand these books and the dominant search term, although whychoose is gaining ground (especially on Tiktok). You'll need to have a look at the debate and the current market and choose for yourself which terms to use. I know that I'm personally moving toward using whychoose more for reader-focused marketing, but for anything requiring keywords and algorithms I'm still using reverse harem.

REVERSE HAREM COVERS

As most reverse harem readers will first notice your book by seeing the cover in a thumbnail on their screen, you need to create a bold design that signals to them that you've hit the right genre.

Begin by compiling a list of your "comp" titles – these are reverse harem books with the same vibe as yours that are doing well RIGHT NOW. For example, for my new release *You're So Dead to Me*, I looked at books doing well in paranormal romance with a lighter, sassier urban fantasy tone (as opposed to the darker books). I tried to stay away from wolf shifters because they're kind of their own thing.

I studied all kinds of things about these books - and I read a bunch to see what readers enjoyed about them. I used this data to inform many things about the writing and packaging of my book.

One thing you can do is place all their covers on a grid and compare them. In the grid format, you can easily see patterns and colors emerging.

Look for elements that are similar between them. What

colors do they use? What motifs are present? How many figures are in the scene? What other objects are present? How is the genre portrayed? What types of font are used for the title and author name?

I could see that in my comp titles, the covers shared a lot of "paranormal" colors in common (purples and blues), they pretty much all had a central female figure, often with a weapon or magical swirls, often some kind of familiar or wolf, swirly, fantastical fonts, an illustrative photomanipulation style, and a clever, magical-sounding title. So I used those elements in my cover.

Your cover grid is also a useful tool to give to your designer so they can design something that incorporates the elements you like.

Why do we do this instead of doing whatever we like for our cover? Because we're writing reverse harem for fun *and money*. Remember before, I said that readers like the same genre and the same experience over and over again? Making your book look similar to others on the market shows them that they will get this same experience they love.

For paranormal reverse harem books, the general trend is for a woman as the central figure. Depending on how the book is written, this figure might be in a power pose with some badass outfit and a weapon, ala urban fantasy.

Or it might be a girl in a beautiful dress. You see these a lot in fairy tale retellings and sometimes in fantasy romance with second-world settings

The magical aspects of the genre might be shown by magical flares and flashes, by animals (to represent shifters), or other clues/props, like a sword.

Fantasy romance is currently having a moment in the charts, which means you'll see a lot more of this style. Fantasy romance novels often either look like old school epic fantasy books (central ½ figures with an epic fantasy scene and maybe some dragons in the background, and swirly fantastical writing), or, more likely, they will be a typography style cover without any figures. These are extremely popular at the moment thanks to Tiktok and you'll see them in all romance genres, but they particularly suit fantasy romance.

For contemporary, the covers are often similar to other contemporary novels. They might include a central figure and some elements to allude to the other tropes – athletic equipment for a sports romance, gates or lockers or a crest for a bully book, etc. Many novels, like CM Stunich's *Filthy Rich Boys*, include only typographic and design elements without a figure.

Dark romance reverse harem will usually have a male on the cover in a grittier, manchest style, or will be typography covers with elements like flowers, skulls, snakes, and objects that suggest powerful men (jewelry/jewels/guns/chess pieces/crowns).

Many covers will also include bare-chested men (manchest). Although manchest covers usually sell high-heat romance novels, they're more difficult to do in reverse harem stories because it's hard to create an attractive composition with all your heroes in the frame. Some people have done it but it's a LOT of nekkid man flesh!

Most RH series will have either one man from the harem on each book, or book one will be the heroine only and subsequent books will feature each man. (See Tate James Madison Kate series and Angel Lawson and Sam Rue's Lords series for examples of how this is done).

Talk to your cover designer about your options and let them work their magic. You hired them to give you a beautiful cover, and they'll come through.

BLURB

As well as hooking readers with the tropes you've used, your blurb needs to alert the reader to the fact your book is reverse harem. The key reason readers turn to reverse harem is because they don't want to read a love triangle where the heroine has to choose. Make this very clear.

The key to a good reverse harem blurb – and it's the same for any blurb – is to go light on the plot details and heavy on the relationship/character conflict. What's the relationship tension? How does the harem factor into the plot? What's the internal conflict the heroine is struggling with and how does this create conflict with the harem?

What are the tropes? I'll say this louder for the people at the back.

WHAT ARE THE TROPES?

Don't be coy about the tropes in your book. If it's a fake relationship, lead with that hook. Is it a stepbrother? Make it obvious from the first paragraph.

Here's an example from my blurb for *Poison Ivy*:

> **I'll do anything to get in. I'll even become theirs.**
> *Victor. Torsten. Cassius – the jock, the artist, the step-brother.*
> *The Poison Ivy Club.*
> *Ruthless.*
> *Connected.*
> *Violent.*
> Untouchable.
> *They rule Stonehurst Prep with an iron fist.*
> *If you want Harvard, Princeton, or Yale, they'll get you in.*

Guaranteed.
But they'll take their pound of flesh first.
A deal's a deal – you give them whatever they want,
    and they'll make your dreams come true.
And they want me.
In their beds.
On their arms.
Part of their gang.
I'll do anything to get into an Ivy League school.
I'll lie. I'll cheat.
I'll get on my knees.
I'll kill.
But those three dark princes will never have my
    heart.
This is a new adult, dark contemporary
    romance with three poisonous guys and one
    fearless girl. It is intended for 18+ readers.

This is one of my most popular books/series ever, and I think in part it's because of this blurb. Why does it work?

a) It's clear from the first paragraph that it's a reverse harem story, that it's a dark bully style, set in high school, and that the heroine has a strong voice.

b) The first line is a strong, bold hook

c) I like to use short, snappy sentences, almost like poems, to create hooks. I try to make it so that every line of the blurb could be used as a teaser and sounds enticing on its own.

d) I have tropes! (The jock, the artist, the stepbrother). I talk about the deal. I tell you there's a secret society and that there's a power imbalance (they rule the school). I let you know that it's in high school and it's dark.

e) I don't waste time in the blurb talking about anything too deep into the book, or even the heroine's name. Plot details are sparse because all I'm doing is trying to get you to pick up the book.

f) What really pulls the reader in is the idea of the deal – they get her into a top college, and she gives herself to them. They want to know what would make someone do this? They like the danger and mystery of it.

g) I use common keywords readers understand as short-hand for the things they like. This blurb doesn't use the words "reverse harem" at all, but you know exactly what it is.

h) I can use that sentence at the bottom to add more information. Telling readers the book is dark is like a neon sign screaming to those dark, depraved souls "this is the book for me!"

It's a good idea to test different blurbs. Testing blurbs is never going to be a perfect science, but you could set up FB ads with two different blurbs and see which one performs better in terms of click-through.

For *The Castle of Earth and Embers*, I've tested two different versions – one in third person, and one in first. Here they are:

Blurb 1:

> **Maeve Crawford has her life mathematically calculated down to the last detail; Leave her podunk Arizona town, graduate MIT, get into the space program, be the first woman on Mars, read lots of books, get a cat (not necessarily in this order).**
>
> All Maeve's careful plans come crashing down when her parents are killed in a freak accident, and she discovers she's inherited a real, honest-to-goodness English castle – complete with turrets, ramparts, and four gorgeous male tenants.

Corbin – the protector wallowing in guilt
Arthur – the warrior tired of fighting
Flynn – the trickster with an artist's soul
Rowan – the enigma whose scars run deep
As soon as Maeve enters Briarwood, she's
drawn to Corbin, Arthur, Flynn, and Rowan
– four beautiful boys drenched in grief,
hope, and ancient magic. Maeve needs
them all to heal her broken heart, and they
need her to help them protect the world
from the fae host baying at the castle gates.
Dark forces converge on Briarwood castle, and
Maeve Crawford – science geek, scarred
soul, lover of four remarkable men – must
draw from herself a power she never imagined in order to protect the shattered
remains of her life.
The Castle of Earth and Embers is the first in
a brand new steamy reverse harem
romance by *USA Today* bestselling author,
Steffanie Holmes. This full-length book
glitters with love, heartache, hope, grief,
dark magic, fairy trickery, steamy scenes,
British slang, meat pies, second chances,
and the healing powers of a good cup of
tea. Read on only if you believe one just
isn't enough.

Blurb 2:

Dear Fae,
Don't even THINK about attacking my
castle.
This science geek witch and her four

magic-wielding men are about to get medieval on your ass.

I'm Maeve Crawford. For years I've had my future mathematically calculated down to the last detail; Leave my podunk Arizona town, graduate MIT, get into the space program, be the first woman on Mars, get a cat (not necessarily in this order).

Then fairies killed my parents and shot the whole plan to hell.

Now, I've inherited a real, honest-to-goodness English castle – complete with turrets, ramparts, and four gorgeous male tenants, who I'm totally not in love with.

Not at all.

It would be crazy to fall for four guys at once, even though they're totally gorgeous and amazing and wonderful and kind.

But not as crazy as finding out I'm a witch. A week ago, I didn't even believe magic existed, and now I'm up to my ears in spells and prophetic dreams and messages from the dead.

It turns out the five of us wield powerful magic that can banish the fae forever. They intend to stop us by killing us all.

I can't science my way out of this mess.

Forget NASA, it's going to take all my smarts just to survive Briarwood Castle.

Earth and Embers is the first in a brand new steamy urban fantasy by USA Today best-selling author, Steffanie Holmes. This full-length book glitters with love, heartache, hope, grief, dark magic, fairy trickery,

steamy scenes, British slang, meat pies,
second chances, and the healing powers of a
good cup of tea. Read on only if you believe
one just isn't enough.

You can see how both blurbs give the same general information, but with a different tone. You may be surprised – or not – to learn that blurb 2 tested better, so that's the blurb I now use. I do most of my blurbs in first person these days because they consistently test better for me, but you might be different.

Read blurbs from other popular reverse harem books and look for patterns. You'll notice hooky first lines, lots of short, snappy sentences, liberal lashings of sexual tension, and a lot of laundry lists (in the same vein as my closing paragraphs). Pay particular attention to the way different authors bring the reverse harem aspect to life and use only a few words to portray a complex relationship.

Don't copy directly (that's shitty and also a copyright violation), but you can use the structure and descriptions in other blurbs as a jumping-off point for your own work.

HITTING THE TROPES

A big part of marketing your reverse harem book is making sure you've hit the tropes that readers are looking for. All the marketing in the world will not make a book rise to the top if it's not something readers want to read. Before you launch, look at your book as a marketer instead of an author, and ask yourself if you need to edit it to make it more appealing to readers. You might also get a friend you trust to read it over and point out how you can improve.

I'm working on a series at the moment which is about a vampire rock band. I finished book one but when I went to write the blurb it was missing something. I took a hard look at the story and realized I'd written a half-arsed fake dating story, but hadn't played up those aspects at all. So now I'm rewriting both the blurb *and* the book to really have fun with that trope.

This may seem weird, but for many of my books, I will write the blurb before I write the actual book. If I can make the blurb work, the book will work. I can see before I write a word if my idea is hooky and fun.

KINDLE UNLIMITED OR WIDE?

Your next big pre-launch consideration is whether you want to enroll your reverse harem book into Kindle Unlimited, or have it available on all stores.

Kindle Unlimited is Amazon's "Spotify for books" program. Readers pay a set monthly fee ($9.99 in the US) to download and read as many books as they want from the KU catalog. Authors who enroll their books in KU are paid a certain amount per page each time a reader turns the page in KU (And the pages are standardized over all books to make it fair). The page rate varies per month but is usually between $0.0040-$0.0048 per page.

Depending on the length of your book and the price you set, you'll usually earn a little less for a full KU-read than you would if the reader purchased the ebook outright.

In order to enroll in Kindle Unlimited, you have to be exclusive to Amazon. Each KU 'term' is for 90 days, so you enroll each book for three months and then you can pull your book out and take it wide if you want. (wide means your book is available "widely" on a number of retailers, but it can't be in KU.)

Kindle Unlimited is only for ebooks, so you can have your ebook enrolled in the programme but your paperbacks and hardcovers (and audiobooks if you do them) can be available everywhere if you want.

Being Amazon-exclusive means you can't have your ebook on sale on iBooks, Kobo, or any other stores. The disadvantage to Kindle Unlimited is that you put all your eggs into one basket. The advantage is that you have access to the vast number of voracious readers who devour reverse harem books in Kindle Unlimited.

For a new author, Kindle Unlimited is a great option, as it gives readers an avenue to 'sample' your writing without having to plonk down their hard-earned cash (as they've already paid for their subscription). The readers feel as though your book is 'free' and so they're more likely to take a chance on a new-to-them author than if they had to pay $2.99+ for your book.

It's up to you whether you enroll your book in Kindle Unlimited or put it on sale across all platforms.

For reverse harem, I strongly recommend you consider Kindle Unlimited for at least the first three months. The vast majority of readers in the genre use this service, and it will help you build an audience. You can always take your books wide later if you find Kindle Unlimited isn't working for you. There are successful wide authors, such as Skye Mackinnon, who has lots of advice on how to take reverse harem books wide. But the majority of authors making the big bucks in reverse harem are in KU.

YOUR BOOK LAUNCH

The most important time for marketing your new reverse harem book is during its launch month. This is when the most eyeballs will be on your book and when Amazon will be promoting it to their audience. Here are some tips to help you rock your reverse harem launch:

TIKTOK

I can't update a romance self-publishing book in 2023 without talking about Tiktok.

The particular part of Tiktok known as "booktok" has become a force of nature in the publishing world, especially for the romance genre. Voracious readers have discovered the platform and are sharing their favorite books far and wide. As an author, you can get your videos in front of those readers and introduce new readers to your work.

Tiktok is currently the **number one source of free traffic for romance authors.** There was a crazy time in 2022 where the top 100 on Amazon was nearly entirely made up of brand-new books that Tiktok had made go viral. Several reverse harem authors owe their success to readers on Tiktok promoting their books for them. Algorithm changes mean this is tougher now, but Tiktok is still an amazing way to promote your books to readers.

So what is Tiktok and how do you use it to find readers? I'm not a Tiktok expert, and I haven't had the kind of wild success many of my colleagues have. But I have definitely found new readers and improved my bottom line by approximately 30% thanks to sustained effort on the platform over the last eighteen months. Here are some things I have learned and tips I can share:

- Tiktok is a video app. There are many different little "spaces" on Tiktok – no matter what kooky hobby you have or videos you like, there is a space on Tiktok for you. I love #poletok and #meadtok (spaces on Tiktok where people share their pole dance videos and their recipes for making mead). One of my friends loves Tiktok videos of people icing cookies. It's a whole thing.

- Booktok is the space on Tiktok for book lovers. The majority of booktok is romance readers, although there are other genre readers there, too. Many of these readers are rediscovering their love of reading thanks to the app, and many of them read hardcovers and paperbacks instead of digital books. My print book sales have increased 700% (no, that's not a typo) since I started on Tiktok.
- You create a free creator account in Tiktok. This is an account only for author stuff, so don't use it to watch random stuff, as that confuses the algorithm. I have a separate account just for watching non-bookish stuff.
- You can have either a Tiktok with your author name (@steffanieholmeswrites) or a passion page about a specific trope (@bullyromancerecs). Passion pages are designed to look like readers recommending books.
- The first thing you should do is train the algorithm to put you in booktok land by following lots of booktok people and liking, saving, and commenting on booktok content on your FYP. Look for readers who post booktok content about your genre (I do this by searching the titles of my comp books or my comp authors on the platform) and follow them. When you're following around 60-80 booktokers, you'll start to be recommended only booktok content in your FYP (For You Page). If I see any non booktok videos on my FYP, I tag them as "not interested".
- You need to decide on a strategy for Tiktok, and be prepared to change that strategy as the algorithm changes, which is every month it seems.

- You can show your face in your videos and talk to readers, do lip syncs and dances to popular sounds, and just be a goof. I do one of these a day because I think it helps readers to get to know me as a person.
- You can also do a type of video called an aesthetic or a "book flip". These are videos with your books displayed in a background (usually with the covers hidden or pages out so people can't see the cover - some research has shown this works better). You may have a candle flickering or be flipping through the pages in a book to create movement. On top of this scene you will overlay a catchy hook or scene from your book. The easiest way to explain these is for you to go and look at them. You can check out my main feed – I do two of these a day for different books.
- You ideally want to be posting once a day, using trending sounds. You can repeat the same hooks/works/videos over and over and over again. I have around 10-20 hooks for each book I keep repeating, often changing the words slightly.
- These aesthetic videos are all about introducing your books to new readers. They often work better on average than videos with your face, although you are not building a following in quite the same way. For this reason I do a mixture of both.
- Keep trying things, and use the FYP to see what others are doing and if you can create your own spin on things. Recently, photo slideshows have been working really well for people, but that might've changed before I publish this book!
- I use a US sim card in a Tiktok-only phone because I live in New Zealand, and Tiktok is currently tied

to your location so it will show your videos to
people in your location first and then they'll go out
to other countries if the algorithm likes them. I am
tricking my phone into thinking I am in the US,
because the majority of my readers are in the US. I
have friends who are in the UK who do fine
without doing this, but New Zealand is a lot
smaller than the UK! It is quite possible that this
isn't working and I'm about to trial using a VPN as
well as my US sim card.

- I do one silly video a day with my face that relates
to my books. I do a lot of book memes and some
lip syncs. I do two aesthetic videos a day and I use
props to make my aesthetics look magical and
mystical.

- You don't have to be perfect! Tiktok is the hot
mess platform. Videos tend to do better when you
show up with no makeup and your hair a total
mess. So don't be afraid to be your authentic self.
Tiktok is so lovely and actually rewards that! It's
really cool.

- Tiktok loves print books and they LOOOOOOVE
object/typography covers, especially if they're a
luxe edition with foil or sprayed edges or other
pretty things. If you have these, show them off in
your vids.

- Tiktok does not care about followers. I have very
few followers and I have still gone viral a couple of
times. Your very first video can go viral. The key is
to pack those videos with tropes that Tiktok loves.

- The best way to find out how to make Tiktok
work for you is to watch heaps of videos, see what
sounds and hooks go viral, and rework them for
your books.

- My *Poison Ivy* book was written based on Tiktok trends. I literally tested scenes in Tiktok videos before I wrote them – if they performed well, I wrote the scene and made it a big deal in the book. If not, I quietly discarded them.
- My last few releases have had a Tiktok campaign that started at least a month in advance promoting the book. Some people start even further out, and have had it pay off. Get people excited for a book even when it's not out yet!

Like I said, I'm not a Tiktok expert, so these are just a few tips to get you started. It's a super fun platform, I absolutely love it, and they are big fans of RH over there. Give it a go, you might be surprised!

If you were going to start with one social media platform for your reverse harem pen name, I'd recommend starting with Tiktok.

INSTAGRAM

Instagram has risen and fallen in popularity over the years. The main feed has been pretty meh for a long time now, but their new feature is reels, which are a Tiktok competitor, and they're worth looking at. I repost my Tiktok videos to reels by using a tool called Snap Tik to remove the Tiktok watermark. I do way better on reels than on Tiktok TBH, but it takes 4 views on a reel to equal 1 view on Tiktok. If I have a video on Tiktok that gets to 5k views, I see a little spike in sales. On Reels, I need to get over 20k views to see the same spike.

Also, the algorithm on reels is not quite as nuanced as Tiktok. I get a lot of mean comments on reels, especially on my darker books. Most of those comments are from people who are very clearly not my audience as they don't like romance novels. So just be aware of that. I don't actually post my dark contemporary books on reels anymore – only my paranormal.

Instagram is a bit more aesthetically focused so images and reels tend to be more polished. I get a lot of followers from Instagram reels and unlike Tiktok, followers do still mean a bit on Insta, so work on putting more fun author content up on your main feed and in your stories to entice them to keep clicking/reading.

FACEBOOK

If you read this book when I first put it out in 2019, I talked a lot about the importance of Facebook. Back then, Facebook was how so many reverse harem readers found their next book to devour. Authors had a huge amount of success by being active in reader groups and by encouraging readers to join their personal author fan groups, where they could tease and tempt readers into picking up their next book.

That's changing. It's become more difficult to gain visibility on Facebook. I have a personal Facebook author group with over 2000 members. When I post, I'm lucky if 10 people see the post unless I use the @everyone tag. But now everyone uses the @everyone tag, which means it will soon be ignored. The large reverse harem reader groups are still there and still active, but they suffer from the same visibility issues, and now that so many more writers are penning RH, the large reader groups are flooded with authors promoting their books. As the actual reader interaction dries up, readers will avoid the groups.

So, Facebook definitely isn't what it once was. But there is still some visibility to be had, and if you're an old millennial like me it's probably the platform you're most comfortable with. The reverse harem Facebook groups are still a great place to introduce yourself to the community, and to network with other authors. I suggest you join some of the biggest groups and apply for a slot for a takeover (this is where you have exclusive posting rights in the group for an hour to introduce readers to your new book). These will help alert readers to your work. They won't be as effective now as they were three years ago, but if you're new to the genre and to self-publishing, those early readers count.

They are also a good place to ask for readers who might be interested in reading an ARC of your book and leaving early reviews.

The more you interact on your author Facebook page or Facebook group, the more your posts will be shown. Welcoming new people to the group, using tags, NOT using links in your posts, and using eye-catching images (I find memes work 100x better than actual promo images, but ymmv.

Also, if you have your own Facebook reader group or page, don't forget to alert them about your release! Your fans want to know when you've written something new, even if not all of them will follow you into reverse harem.

You can also use Facebook to run ads targeting new readers. Facebook ads are a steep learning curve and I would recommend holding off on using them until you have a deeper understanding of the genre and your goals as an author – focus on getting the packaging of your book right first and getting all the bits and bobs in place (a mailing list, your social media, etc).

I am not a FB ads expert and I have someone who runs these for me. So I won't give any advice on them here. But you can find lots of great books, courses, and groups out there that will teach you how to rock them.

MAILING LIST

If you don't already have a mailing list, now is a good time to set one up. Most writers use services like Mailerlite or Mailchimp, however there are literally hundreds to choose from. I use a company called ConvertKit and I love them because it's all quite simple and there aren't lots of bells and whistles but it still does a lot.

Once your list is set up, link it in the back of your book, and readers will sign up to be alerted when you have a new release. I like to offer readers an exclusive scene or free story in exchange for their email address. This helps encourage more people to sign up.

I write a bonus piece of content for (nearly) every new series I write. I add each scene to a free book I have called the *Cabinet of Curiosities*. This is what readers get when they sign up to the newsletter. So they don't just get their bonus scene, but all the other bonus scenes. I have links to each book 1 in the bonus scenes and I can see that readers click on those links from this book, so it does help a bit with sell-through between series.

What kinds of bonus content can you write? I've tried everything – I have epilogues set after the HEA (mainly on my standalone non-RH older books), prologue stories set in the past, alternative POV scenes where you take a scene from the book and rewrite it from another character's POV, and even writing scenes that take place in the book but are talked about but not witnessed by any of the POV characters. I've also done fun lists (Heathcliff's Bookshop Rules from Nevermore Bookshop) and Spotify playlists.

Alternative POV scenes are my favorites – they take the least effort to write and readers love them, especially if they give more insight into the POV of the heroes.

Most readers join my mailing list from the link in the

back of my books (right underneath the TO BE CONTIN-UED, after I've linked to the pre-order for the next book), and from the pop up on my website.

If you already have readers on your mailing list, then you should alert them about your new release. About 6-8 weeks before release, I show them the cover and blurb. About a month before release, basically from the time I have a decent first draft, I start sending out weekly excerpts. I might also send funny lists or little "did you know" things about the books. I have a lot of fun basically trying to convince the readers they HAVE to read this book.

You can also ask other authors to promote your book to their lists. We call this a 'newsletter swap'. It's most effective if the audience for your book and the other author's books is as close as possible. I have a few long-term author friends who I swap with on a regular basis and it always adds a wee boost. This can take a bit of organizing but it can be a simple thing you can do to start promoting your book as a newer RH author.

Pro tip: If you already have romance novels out and an extensive list of readers before you started publishing RH, keep a separate list or group within your main list of readers who enjoy reverse harem. When I first started writing RH, I would send out newsletters to this list first, before my larger list. Doing this helped Amazon to learn that my books are similar to other reverse harem books, and meant that I'm more likely to be advertised alongside other reverse harem titles in also-boughts and in searches. Nowadays, my list is all the same, but back when I started it was good to do.

AMS ADS

AMS ads are pay-per-click ads operated by Amazon. They allow you to bid against other authors for better placement in search results, in the 'sponsored products' section located on each book product page, and on the lockscreens of Kindles.

AMS ads can take a lot of fiddling to figure out. Your first step is to compile keyword lists of book titles, authors, and keyword searches related to your books. Look for similar reverse harem authors and reverse harem keywords – you'll be familiar with the concept of looking for "comp authors" from the beginning of this section. These comp authors will be useful here. Once you have this list, you can test different ads with a small budget ($3-5 per day). Over time you will start to notice what works and what doesn't.

Be aware that Amazon does not allow the words 'reverse harem', 'harem', 'alpha', and any description that implies your book contains a polyamorous relationship in your AMS ad copy. This includes the title, series title, and subtitle of your book and on your cover. It often includes the blurb, too.

You'll need to consider if it's worthwhile for you to include 'reverse harem' on your cover or in your series name. My Briarwood Witches series was originally called 'Briarwood Reverse Harem' but I changed it so I could run AMS ads (which I haven't found very effective, so I'm not certain the change was worthwhile).

Again, I'm not an Amazon ads expert so I won't chime in with tips. I currently don't run these ads, but there are heaps of awesome people out there with books and courses and groups to help you.

GIVEAWAYS

In the early days of RH, I had success running themed giveaways based on details from my books. For example, I ran a mega giveaway to celebrate the final book release in the Briarwood Witches series. I included a gift from every character in the harem that suited their personality. Candles, tarot cards, necklaces, etc, as well as signed copies of all the books.

I used the site King Sumo (kingsumo.com) to set up the giveaway. I usually run them for 3-4 weeks. On King Sumo, participants can get additional entries for completing different tasks. I offer additional entries for people who visit the book's page on Amazon, sign up for my mailing list, join my author group, and follow me on Instagram. Each time I run one, I add a few hundred new people on each of those platforms.

I send these giveaways out to my mailing list and promote them on my Facebook page/group and on my blog. You could also use Instagram and Tiktok to promote them, too. I also ask other authors if I can add the giveaway on their Facebook groups. Then I can announce the release of my new book on those platforms and capture readers' attention.

This might be a simple thing you can do to introduce readers to your new reverse harem book or series. Another thing you might also try is giving away paperbacks of your book alongside paperbacks of other bestselling RH authors that are similar – this will draw on their readers who want to win and show them your book is similar.

Chapter Five

BUILDING YOUR AUDIENCE

If you want to keep releasing reverse harem books, then it helps to have an audience of eager readers ready to snap them up.

Your reverse harem audience will build over time as you release more books and word gets around the community about how awesome you are.

However, there are things you can do to help build and maintain that audience of fans, so that they're excited about your next release and actively spreading the word about your awesomeness. I've found this the most effective marketing strategy for growing my profile in reverse harem – especially important when you don't have a huge advertising budget to throw around.

NEWSLETTER

As discussed in the previous section, your newsletter is a valuable tool for capturing fans and alerting them about new releases. However, you can also use it as a tool for connecting with your fans by mailing out fun teasers, competitions and giveaways, behind-the-scenes author stuff, and fun games and trivia. Sending to your newsletter regularly keeps you front of mind to your fans (many of whom read a book a day and forget about authors between releases) and make sure they definitely absolutely know that you have a new book coming out.

I firmly believe that my newsletter is my most valuable marketing tool because I own that data. With social media sites, you might do really well but then they change an algorithm or ban you for no reason and then you can't get those followers back. But with email you can move your list around different services.

Use the tools provided by your mailing list service to test how often you can send your newsletter and which types of content are most popular. Compare open rates and click-through rates (click-through rates are a more accurate representation these days) and create a schedule that works for you.

Personally, I try to send one once a week. I find that with so many books out and a new release approximately every two months, I always have something to share.

What kinds of things can you post in your reader group?

- Teasers from your upcoming release. Probably 50% of the newsletters I send are some kind of teaser.
- Cover reveals/blurb reveals.
- Announcements (new releases, pre-orders, paperbacks available, appearances at signings, etc).
- Playlists and songs that relate to your books.
- Fun facts about your books. This is another thing I love to do. My books contain a lot of literary references and historical factoids, so I like to draw readers into those with short profiles about them.

- Behind-the-scenes in your writer cave. I also like to do this. These days I do a lot of Tiktok videos so I post links to these.
- Pictures of your pets (these are always popular).
- Tracking your word count goals. I think this is less exciting for readers than teasers, but it can also be a way for them to see that a book they're excited about is coming soon.
- 5 things you didn't know about my upcoming book (this is one of my favorite things to write)
- Promo for other authors' books you think your readers will like. The bonus is that if a lot of your readers pick up a book from another author, you might appear in their also-bots, and that can be good for you.
- Surveys/polls about your books. Anything that gets readers to click will massively improve your newsletter engagement and mean more people will see your newsletter.
- New audiobooks!
- When paperbacks go live!
- Competitions and things to win (another way to get readers to click)

There are companies who run "newsletter builders" where they will use competitions to create a list of readers who like your genre, and you can then add those readers to your email list. I would keep these readers on a separate list to your "organic" subscribers (subscribers who've signed up to your list after reading one of your books) and I'd give these list-builder readers a welcome sequence to introduce them to your books (because they have no idea who you are). When you're starting out, sometimes doing lots of list-builders and having a solid welcome sequence (perhaps with a sample) can be a great way to get an audience before you release.

Over time, you may see that those subscribers aren't valuable to you or actually harm your newsletter's deliverability. I've used them in the past but for about 5 years now I've had a solely organic list. It's smaller than other authors at my level, but it is highly interactive with high deliverability.

SOCIAL MEDIA

As well as a newsletter, it's good to have someplace online for readers to congregate for updates and fun, as well as a free way to put your book in front of new readers. Social media is often this place – it's the best free source to find new readers in your genre and turn them into fans. But "free" is relative, because it takes time to do social media well.

In reverse harem, many authors began with Facebook as their dominant form of social media, and they use it to participate in big genre reader groups and to run their own reader groups. In these reader groups, authors post about book progress, tease covers and excerpts, talk about random facts related to the book, ask questions, run polls, do giveaways, and play silly games. In larger groups, the author might have a PA who posts memes and games and manages comments, to keep the engagement up in the group when the author can't post all the time.

I'll be honest here – Facebook groups were amazing in 2019, but they're significantly less amazing now. It's difficult to get any visibility without using the @everyone tag, but now everyone uses this tag, so it's only a matter of time before readers start ignoring it. Some authors with large, highly engaged groups still find them valuable, but I'm not sure if I would put my energy into a Facebook group at the moment.

Where would I put my energy? As of this writing, probably Tiktok or Instagram reels, but that could change on a dime.

My recommendation with social media is to choose one platform that you enjoy and "get", and then focus on doing that platform as well as you possibly can. Pour your energy into it. You might later add a second platform, especially if there's a benefit to cross-posting (for example, most authors cross-post their Tiktoks to reels). And then work on funneling readers into platforms where you control the data, like a newsletter or Patreon.

BOX SETS AND COLLECTIONS

As you publish more books in your series, you're able to bundle them together into collections and boxsets. You can sell these boxsets as additional products on Amazon (and other platforms if you're wide), and they're a great tool for attracting readers and re-igniting interest in a flagging series.

The best time to release a boxset is when sales/page reads on the single titles begin to flag. Because you offer the boxset at a discount (my 5-book Briarwood Witches box set is $9.99, whereas the individual books are $4.99 each), the box set sales can sometimes cannibalize interest in the other books.

You can offer a box set of the entire series or – if it's a longer series – just the first three books, with another set for the next 3 – creating another series of sets.

If you have a lot of different series, you might like to create a 'starter library' box set of the first books in all your different series.

MULTI-AUTHOR BOX SETS

Multi-author box sets are when a group of authors gets together to create a box set. These sets usually sell for $0.99 and offer readers 10-20 novels – one each from the participating authors. Each author will then get the chance to promo the next book in their series or another release at the end of their novel.

Multi-author box sets are a great deal for readers because they get so many books for such a low price, and they might discover new authors to follow. For authors, they offer you the chance to get your name in front of a large number of new readers.

As Amazon tightens the rules around these sets, multiauthor box sets have waned in popularity. However, since 2017 there have been several reverse harem sets that have done exceptionally well. You may like to consider a box set as an option to expand your readership or promote a popular series.

Be wary of box set coordinators who make their business out of recruiting authors for sets, especially those who promise 'USA Today bestseller" status. A lot of these have disappeared now that the USA Today bestseller list is on hiatus. Basically, if the goal of a set is to hit a list, the organizers will encourage a lot of tactics that are aimed at getting as many sales as possible (eg. giving your family and friends money to purchase the set, buy-swaps with other authors, etc) but these sales aren't from actual readers. And that should be the whole goal of a set - to reach new readers!

Most box sets will be in Kindle Unlimited, and they will require you to submit a novel that is not only exclusive to Amazon, but exclusive to the box set (for a limited time). Some authors will unpublish their first-in-series book for a limited time in order to place that in the box set. However, this may confuse readers who stumble on your series but can't find book one, so I'd probably write something new instead.

More commonly, authors will submit a new work – usually the first book in a new series. They might use the box set as a way to 'test' the market for a new series idea. They may write a short novella and then expand that idea into a novel later if there's enough reader interest. They may write a prequel to an as-yet unpublished series.

Alternatively, an author might write a spin-off novella or novel featuring characters in an already-established series.

If you're submitting a book to a box set, look for sets that are exclusively for reverse harem novels. This ensures you're targeting the most relevant audience. Look for sets that focus on reaching as many readers as possible as their primary goal. You want to introduce yourself to new readers, who may go on to read the rest of your series.

Participating in a multi-author box set is a lot of work. You'll be expected to perform duties like advertising the set and participating in group promos. You may also pay a fee in order to be part of the set (this fee will cover paid promotion of the set). Make sure you have the time and money to commit before jumping in, and that your set owner operates a professional set with contracts and acceptable terms. Authors have been caught out by box-set scammers and unprofessional presentations before, so ask around about the reputation of the set organizer, trust your instincts, and keep everything in writing.

These days, I'm very picky about sets. I pretty much only participate in sets organized by friends when I'm invited. Writing for a set can take time away for your main writing schedule, for a smaller payoff. But they can be great when you're new to a genre. You may also like to organize your own set, but be aware that it's a lot of work!

MERCH/WEBSTORE

With Tiktok fueling a surge in reader love for signed, limited edition, fancypants books, many reverse harem authors are opening their own online stores. These stores will sell signed and unsigned paperbacks and hardcovers, special edition covers, audiobooks (usually delivered through Bookfunnel), fun merchandise like t-shirts, artwork and stickers related to the series, and sometimes limited edition book boxes.

Many authors are doing well with their webstores – Britt Andrews has a fabulous one, as does AK Rose. I'm launching mine soon at www.nevermorebookshop.com and I'm so excited!

Online stores serve two purposes – 1. They're an extra income stream and 2. They expand the world of your books through physical products, so they are a great way to encourage fandom for your books/series.

Just remember that an online store requires a huge amount of effort to source products, ship, manage inventory, deal with customer service, etc. I'm only doing one because I'm at a point in my career where I can hire someone to manage it for me, but this obviously means the store has to have enough traffic to cover her salary and make me some money.

IN-PERSON READER EVENTS

Many reverse harem writers enjoy meeting their readers in real life at signing events and conventions.

When considering in-person events, carefully weigh up cost/benefit to make sure you're going to get value for money. Some events ask you to sponsor reader swag or give away a certain amount of books. Others require you to stay at a specific hotel that might add significantly to your costs. As a self-published author, you'll also be paying to print and ship boxes of your books for signings. It's important that all this investment is recouped. Don't just sign up for events to appease your own vanity about being an invited author – put that money toward top-notch covers and editing for your next release.

Always ask yourself, will this event deepen my relationship with my readers? What am I gaining by participating? How many readers will actually show up? Events aren't really about growing readership – they're more about encouraging fandom by meeting fans and giving them a cool experience of having their books signed in front of them by their favorite author.

I've started going to a few author signing events – RARE events in Australia and Europe, and the BABE event in Australia. They are so much fun! I have lots of tips on what to do (and what not to do), but that's a whole other topic for a different book!

SUBSCRIPTIONS

A subscription like Patreon is a way for fans to "subscribe" to a monthly payment in exchange for cool extras. As a fan of an author, I might pay $5 a month for behind-the-scenes updates and NSFW artwork, or $15 a month to read a book a chapter-at-a-time (serial fiction) as the author writes it.

Many reverse harem authors are turning to Patreon as a way to build an additional income stream from giving extra content to super fans. You can create different tiers - fans will pay more for cool stuff. It's basically like having an old school fan club, which I totally love.

Common rewards authors offer to their Patreon tiers include:

- ARC copies of books.
- Audiobook codes.
- A blog of behind-the-scenes updates.
- SFW and NSFW artwork.
- A monthly bonus scene (usually something steamy).
- The ability to vote on upcoming artwork or upcoming bonus scenes.
- Serialised fiction (usually exclusive to Patreon).
- Patreon-exclusive limited editions, special book boxes, and other merch.
- A discount code for your online store.
- First chance at new merch in your store.
- Character interviews and other fun bonus content.
- Q&A live streams, podcasts, or threads.

The thing about Patreon is that it's not a platform for finding new fans. It is a way to engage with fans you already have. So it works best once you have established yourself. But if it's something you're into, you might like to build it early so it's there when you have a book take off. Check out other author patreons to see how they do it. One of my favorites is Nikki St Crowe – that woman is amazing!

The other thing to remember about Patreon is that you have to keep adding content monthly, even if you only have a couple of patrons. So you need to create a model that's sustainable for you. Don't bite off more than you can chew because you're committing to this for the long haul!

(I'm thinking of launching a Patreon later this year. Mine will not be including any physical rewards at this stage because the effort of organizing them and shipping them from NZ isn't worth it. I will have only three tiers. A cheap tier with updates and artwork. A mid-level tier with bonus content and other fun stuff, and an author tier for writing and self-publishing advice.

There's another awesome tool out called Ream – this is an author-centric alternative to Patreon (Patreon is for all kinds of creatives - I back a lot of musicians on it). Ream is mainly about serial fiction a la Wattpad, and it is seriously awesome. A lot of authors are starting to launch and switch over there – something to consider if your subscription is going to be about serializing fiction and releasing books early.

Chapter Six

WHAT NEXT?

Now that you've released your reverse harem book and you're growing your audience, what should you do next?

WRITE THE NEXT BOOK

The sooner you finish the second book in your reverse harem series (you are writing a series, aren't you?) the more likely you are to capture those hungry readers before they forget about the story.

Many reverse harem writers (myself included) are publishing books at the rate of one every 8 weeks. Some are even faster.

If you write between 1-4 books a year, you can make a significant improvement to your bottom line by growing your yearly output by one book. For example, if you would normally publish one book a year, if you can increase it to two, you will likely see a decent income jump. Ditto from two books to three, and from three to four. After this, income jumps tend to come from other factors, such as running ads and building a fandom. (My best year so far was a year I published 4 books instead of my usual 6-8, but that's the power of a hit series, and you never know which series will hit).

Getting onto that next book quickly (and not being distracted by new shiny things) is a good way to keep your momentum going.

You should go at your own pace and write a story that's compelling, but you may like to investigate ways to increase your daily word count to improve your speed.

Pro tip: Rachel Aaron has a great book called *2k to 10k: Writing Faster, Writing Better, and Writing More of What You Love* about increasing your word count that might be useful.

INTERACT WITH READERS

Between book releases, keep reader interest alive by posting regularly in your author group, sending out newsletters, and using the other tools and tips we talked about in the previous section. Make sure no one has time to forget your name!

GROW YOUR GROUP/NEWSLETTER

Use bonus scenes, giveaways, regular content, author takeovers, and paid promotions to grow your email list, reader group, and social media. If you can increase these numbers between launches, you can improve sales of your series as you add more books.

EXPAND YOUR OFFERED FORMATS

You've got your books out in ebook and paperback, but once you're earning a bit of money, you might like to reinvest in your business by putting your reverse harem books into different formats. This gives you more products to sell to grow your audience while making the most of the IP you've already created.

The most common formats you can try are audiobooks and translations. I have some of my most popular books in audiobook format, and I'm currently expanding into German and Italian translations. You'll need funds upfront to pay for an audiobook narrator or translator, so you need to be certain that you can recoup that money in sales. That's why I recommend only going this route once you're earning a decent amount in English. It provides funds and it gives you an idea of which books are hitting the market well and will likely earn out.o

You have other options, too. Nikki St. Crowe is turning her Vicious Lost Boys series into a graphic novel. Many authors have their books made into games and interactive fiction on various apps. You may even end up being the first reverse harem author to have a movie or TV show made!

TRY A SALE

Once you have more than three books in your reverse harem series, you might like to experiment with putting book one on sale for a few days. If your book is enrolled in Kindle Unlimited, you can schedule up to 5 free days during every 3-month period, or a countdown deal where you can price your book at $0.99 and keep 70% royalties (as opposed to the 35% you'd normally expect at that price point).

If your book is wide, you can set your books to free on the other platforms and wait for Amazon to price-match it, and you can set a sales amount for $0.99.

You may like to use newsletter services like FreeBooksy, Bookbub, Robin Reads, and Red Feather Romance to promote your sale.

HAVE FUN!

Don't lose sight of why you're writing and publishing reverse harem – because it's fun and because you have unique stories to tell.

I've never been happier than when I've been exploring the worlds I've created and the remarkable characters who inhabit them. I love the challenge of making everyone smoosh booties and overcome obstacles to achieve their happily ever after.

Reverse harem is regular romance on steroids. We get to explore a fascinating relationship dynamic and write about strong, sassy women who command the devotion of amazing men. We get to be fantasy-spinners and dream-makers, and it's damn cool.

So what are you waiting for? Get started on your reverse harem romance novel today!

Chapter Seven

WANT TO LEARN HOW TO ROCK YOUR AUTHOR BRAND?

Rock Your Author Brand: https://www.
rageagainstthemanuscript.com/rockauthorbrand
Get $20 off with the REVERSEHAREM coupon.

Are you self-publishing your books but feel like you aren't making progress?
Are you doing ALL THE THINGS - social media, ads, promo - but aren't seeing the success you crave?
Do you struggle to find ways to market your books?
Do you want to earn more royalties, write books readers love, and build an army of superfans?

If you want to get strategic about self-publishing, write books readers CRAVE, market them effectively without going crazy, and make MONEY from your books, this is the course for you.

We are going to clear away all the bollocks that's holding you back and stressing you out and focus on what gets YOUR books into the hands of YOUR readers.

First, I'm going to help you **define your author brand**

in a way that makes sense to you as an author. No marketing jargon here, we're going to talk about branding in terms that have meaning to you.

Next, we're going to take your brand and apply it to the **research, writing, publishing, and marketing of your books**, using a specific method that I use to streamline my decision-making and cut out the guff that isn't working.

All of this to achieve our ultimate goal – sell more books. Turn readers into superfans. Take over the world.

The course covers:

- **Exactly WHAT is an author brand?** I give you a definition of branding that's author-centric, simple, and easy-to-apply to your entire author biz.
- **Discover the self-publishing income formula.** I lay out exactly how self-publishers earn a sustainable income and give you a formula to help you hit your goals.
- **Trends, tropes, and reader expectations.** We look at how to study the market, define trends, research tropes, and how to decide what to write next.
- **Covers, editing, and blurbs.** Learn the importance of book packaging and how to make your books into reader CRACK.
- **Marketing, social media, and engaging superfans.** Learn to create a marketing plan for your books based on your brand, navigate tools like social media, and engage and inspire your superfans.
- **Putting it all together.** You'll learn how to create a strategy for your writing, publishing and marketing based on your brand and hit your income goals.

Are you ready to get clear on who you are as an author, what you're writing, who your readers are, and how to get your books in front of them? Learn about studying the market, building a self-publishing strategy, and choosing the marketing that will work for you.

Rock Your Author Brand will show you how to develop in-depth strategy to build a successful pen name and author brand: https://www.rageagainstthemanuscript.com/rockauthorbrand

Get $20 off with the REVERSEHAREM coupon.

Chapter Eight

REVERSE HAREM READING LIST

I've compiled this list of some of my favorite reverse harem books, many of which I've mentioned in this guide.

In order to effectively write in any genre, you need to understand its conventions and tropes, so you know what readers want. If you haven't already devoured several reverse harem books, I suggest you choose a few titles off this list and get started:

SOME OF MY TITLES

Steffanie Holmes, Briarwood Witches series (paranormal witches/fae)

Book 1, *The Castle of Earth and Embers*.

Steffanie Holmes, Nevermore Bookshop Mysteries series (paranormal literary heroes)

Book 1, *A Dead and Stormy Night*.

. . .

Steffanie Holmes, Stonehurst Prep: Elite series (dark bully/gang/mafia)

>Book 1, *Poison Ivy*

Steffanie Holmes, Kings of Miskatonic Prep series (dark bully/paranormal)

>Book 1, *Shunned*

BY OTHER AUTHORS

Nikki St. Crowe, Vicious Lost Boys (dark fantasy peter pan retelling)

>Book 1, *The Never King*

Raven Kennedy, Plate Prisoner series (dark fantasy King Midas retelling)

>Book 1, *Gild*

Angel Lawson and Samantha Rue, Royals of Forsyth U (dark bully/gang/mafia contemporary)

>Book 1, *Lords of Pain*

Tate James, Madison Kate series (dark contemporary/gang)

>Book 1, *Hate*

Bethany Jadin, The Code series (action, romantic suspense)

>Book 1, *Vested Interest.*

. . .

Marie Robinson, Beautiful Secrets series (paranormal, fairy-tale retelling)
    Book 1, *House of Secrets*.

CM Stunich, Rock Hard Beautiful series (contemporary rockstar)
    Book 1, *Groupie*.

CM Stunich, The Havoc Boys series (dark contemporary bully/gang)
    Book 1, *Havoc at Prescott High*

Bea Paige, Academy of Stardom series (dark bully, gang contemporary at dance school)
    Book 1, *Freestyle*

KT Strange, Rogue Witch series (paranormal rockstar)
    Book 1, *Phoenixcry*.

B L Brunnemer, Veil Diaries (paranormal young adult)
    Book 1, *Trying to Live With The Dead*.

CL Stone, Scarab Beetle series (young adult)
    Book 1, *Thief*.

Tate James, Kit Davenport series (paranormal)
    Book 1, *Vixen's Lead*.

. . .

Jaymin Eve, Curse of the Gods series (paranormal gods)
    Book 1, *Trickery*.

Kristy Cunning, All The Pretty Monsters series (paranormal vampire)
    Book 1, *Gypsy Blood*.

Eva Chase, Witch's Consorts series (paranormal gothic)
    Book 1, *Consort of Secrets*.

Eva Chase, Gang of Ghosts series (paranormal ghosts with psycho heroes)
    Book 1, *The Stalking Dead*

Eva Chase, Shadowblood Souls series (paranormal urban fantasy monsters psycho men)
    Book 1, *Shattered Vow*

Joely Sue Burkhart, Their Vampire Queen series (paranormal vampire)
    Book 1, *Queen Takes Knights*.

Alex Liddell, Power of Five series (paranormal fae)
    Book 1, *Power of Five*.

. . .

Reese Rivers, The Masked Duet (contemporary college angsty romance)
 Book 1, *Dance Butterfly Dance*

Sam Hall, The Wolfverse (fated mates wolf shifter paranormal)
 Wolf in Sheep's Clothing

Katie May, Prodigium Academy (dark paranormal academy)
 Book 1, *Monsters*

RL Caulder, Blood Oath series (dark paranormal vampires)
 Book 1, *Rite of Loyalty*

HOW TO ROCK SELF-PUBLISHING

- Do you have a story you're bursting to tell the world?
- Are you sick of being rejected by the publishing establishment?
- Do you want to inject a little punk rock, DIY ethos into your indie author career?

In *How to Rock Self-Publishing*, bestselling indie author and publishing coach Steff Green shows you how to tell your story, find your readers, and build a badass author brand.

As a self-published author you'll learn how to:

- Define your measure of success and set attainable goals.
- Create an exciting author brand you want to write under forever.
- Tame your monkey mind and consolidate your gazillion ideas into a solid plan.
- Choose the best platforms, editors, designers, and tools to create a high-quality book.

- Plan a compelling book series in any genre that will have your readers chomping for more.
- Write faster, release more often, and enjoy what you create.
- Spot trends and gaps in the market where you can add your unique voice.
- Publish your book in print, ebook, and audio with all the nuts and bolts.
- Launch with a BANG! – including handy launch checklists.
- Create an engaging author platform to turn your readers into lifelong fans.
- Find unique and emerging opportunities in self-publishing to build your audience and earn a living.

Steff breaks down the 11-step process that's seen her go from failed archaeologist and obscure music blogger to a *USA Today* bestseller with a six-figure income. With dozens of examples from across the publishing landscape and real-talk from her own career, Steff shows how imagination, creativity, and perseverance can help you achieve your dreams.

How to Rock Self-Publishing isn't just a book about writing, it's about grabbing your dreams by the balls, living faster, harder and louder, and cranking your art up to 11.

Read now

ABOUT THE AUTHOR

Steffanie Holmes writes steamy paranormal romance with a touch of the gothic. She's the award-winning and bestselling author of more than 50 books, including the popular reverse harem series – Kings of Miskatonic Prep and the Nevermore Bookshop Mysteries.

In 2017, Steff was awarded the Attitude Award for Artistic Achievement, in recognition of her work as a writer with a disability. In 2018 she was a finalist for a New Zealand woman of influence.

Before becoming a writer, Steffanie worked as an archae-ologist and museum curator. She loves to explore myth, magic, and ancient conceptions of love. From Dark Age Europe to crumbling gothic estates, Steffanie is fascinated with how love can blossom between the most unlikely characters.

Steffanie lives in New Zealand with her husband and a horde of cantankerous cats.

Come hang with Steffanie
www.steffanieholmes.com
hello@steffanieholmes.com